John S. Blackie, Theodor Körner

War Songs of the Germans

With historical illustrations of the Liberation war and the Rhine boundary question

John S. Blackie, Theodor Körner

War Songs of the Germans

With historical illustrations of the Liberation war and the Rhine boundary question

ISBN/EAN: 9783337383992

Printed in Europe, USA, Canada, Australia, Japan

Cover: Foto ©ninafisch / pixelio.de

More available books at **www.hansebooks.com**

WAR SONGS
OF THE GERMANS

With Historical Illustrations

OF

THE LIBERATION WAR

AND THE RHINE BOUNDARY QUESTION

BY JOHN STUART BLACKIE

PROFESSOR OF GREEK

EDINBURGH
EDMONSTON AND DOUGLAS
1870.

TO

THOMAS CARLYLE, Esq.

MY OLD AND ESTEEMED FRIEND,—You and I have had many stiff battles about not a few things; but in two points I have always felt that we are at one—in a stern love of justice, and a hearty detestation of all sickly sentiment. From these two fundamental instincts it has no doubt arisen, that on the subject of the political relations between France and Germany for the last four hundred years, we have arrived, by independent roads, at precisely the same conclusion. It was therefore with peculiar pleasure that I received your kind permission to grace with your name the three chapters in prose and verse which I here put forth on this important theme. They consist of two articles on the great German Liberation War in 1813, originally published in *Tait's Magazine* thirty years ago, and an additional article on the important question of the Rhine Boundary, on the history of which all educated men at the present moment ought to be well informed. These articles are mere fragments of a work on the Liberation War, for which I had collected large materials, at a time when Providence had not yet marked out for me a less genial, but more useful sphere of action. Fragmentary as they are, however, I am confident they will not be found superficial; and I trust also they may prove such as not to be altogether unworthy of a kindly approval from a man who, more, perhaps, than any one now living, knows what honest work means. May you long continue to hold forth in your life and writings, to all English-speaking men, a noble example of that manly independence, lofty fervour, and unbribed truthfulness, without which the greatest literary successes are mere painted flowers, and the honours which vulgar ambition covets a dress which smothers the frame that it should adorn.

<blockquote>
Believe me,

MY DEAR CARLYLE,

Yours, with sincere esteem,

JOHN STUART BLACKIE.
</blockquote>

24 HILL STREET, EDINBURGH,
November 23, 1870.

CONTENTS.

	PAGE
I.—SONGS OF THE-LIBERATION WAR,	1
1. Es zog aus Berlin ein tapferer Held,	25
2. Was ist des Deutschen Vaterland?	30
3. Was Blasen die Trompeten?	51
II.—A NICHE FOR KÖRNER,	58
4. Was Glaenzt dort vom Walde?	72
5. Vater, ich rufe Dich!	78
6. Du Schwert an meiner Linken,	80
III.—THE RHINE BOUNDARY,	85
7. Sie sollen ihn nicht haben,	125
8. Die Wacht am Rhein,	128
9. Am Rhein, am Rhein, da wachsen unsre Reben,	132
Appendix of German Words to the Melodies,	136

WAR SONGS.

I.

SONGS OF THE LIBERATION WAR.

Was wir gehört, gelesen
Tritt wirklich in die Zeit,
Gewinne jetzt ein Wesen
Auch du Gelehrsamkeit!
    SCHENKENDORF.

Ecce quam bonum,
Bonum et jucundum,
Ceciderunt hostes,
Hostes sunt fusi!
    BURSCHEN SONG.

Quoi! les Prussiens à Paris?—BERANGER.

NAPOLEON was driven out of Germany, in the year 1813, mainly by three things: first, he was unhorsed by Boreas in the north; and, though he was ready to reply to the eager questioning of Europe, like a certain Modern Athenian, on occasion of a similar mischance—'Hurt! Oh no, QUITE THE CONTRARY, my Lord!' yet the fact is that he was hurt, and that seriously, in more ways than one. The least of his misfortunes was, that he was obliged to borrow a clean shirt from the King of Saxony when he came

A

to Dresden; the greatest, that he was shorn of glory, robbed of the prestige of victory. The '*On ne peut pas!*' that limits the successes of common humanity, was now publicly declared valid, in certain cases, against Napoleon also. Wagram had blotted out the memory of Aspern; but here was something worse than Aspern—something more ominous than a sullen retreat into a small island of the Danube (a mishap which sappers and pontoons might repair and did repair); here was rout, flight, total overthrow, anticipated annihilation. Besides, the wings of the French eagle actually were terribly mangled in that rude conflict; and, though they grew again, and looked very fair, with a rapidity and a lustihood which showed that the genius of a magician was still there, yet they were not so strong as the old ones. Conscripts could never be veterans; the '*cochons du lait*,' as Marshal Ney knew, might 'fight like devils;' but they could neither create cavalry for the Emperor nor food for themselves. In the second place, these things happened in the face—say rather at the feet—of Prussia; and the Prussia of 1813 was neither the Prussia of 1806 nor the Prussia of 1809. The Countess de Voss, first lady of honour to her Prussian Majesty, in the year 1808, received from an English officer, who had been in the West Indies, a most beautiful parrot, which amused the royal family greatly, by repeating, fifty times a day, as if to prevent mistake, GOD DAMN NAPOLEON. ('Oh, the charming parrot!' says the Countess.[1]) But this was all the length that Frederick William's patriotism was willing or able to go at that time. In 1813, however, Europe was to be taught at last that the Prussian eagle was indeed an eagle, a legitimate consanguinean of the other imperial birds; Blücher, Gneisenau, and Scharnhorst had been nursing hate and brewing thunder for seven indignant years: with them, also, the whole Prussian people were aflame; a PEOPLE verily (thanks to Stein and Hardenberg), not an ARMY merely, as in Frederick's days. This was what Napoleon did not calculate upon; and this, much more than the Russian robbing of the prestige, was the cause of the victories of Katzbach, Gross Beeren, Dennewitz, Culm, and Wartenburg, without which it is quite certain that Leipzig never could have been fought. The third thing that damaged Napoleon in 1813—hemming him round, as it were, with certain destruction—was the accession of Austria to the Russo-Prussian alliance, after the armistice of Poischwitz. This armistice the conqueror had been forced to enter into, as into that of Znaym, in 1809, by the determined resistance which he had

---

[1] *Anecdotes of Foreign Courts* (London, 1827), vol. i. p. 264.

met with from his enemies in two successive battles of fearful carnage and no plunder. Lützen and Bautzen were as honourable to the Prussians as Aspern and Wagram were to the Austrians. Napoleon beat his adversaries off the ground in both cases; but his loss was equal to theirs—his gain merely nominal; the spirit of the adversary unsubdued; and the fruits to be gathered depending altogether upon the general pacific or warlike policy of the party with whom he had to deal. The Prussians, in 1813, were not in a temper to be either cozened or bullied. It does not appear that they were strong enough to have conquered the great god of battles without the Austrians: with the Austrians their victory was certain; and, whatever the thorough-going advocates of Napoleon may say, it does not seem in anywise unreasonable that the gigantic genius of war, overstriding the world in thunder, should be opposed by the only might which common mortals can bring against such dæmonian manifestations—superiority in the quality of moral enthusiasm, and in the quantity of cannonballs.

It is really a pitiful thing to observe how biographers of great men, like the preachers of sectarian gospels, are not content that their hero be gigantic, unless they prove also that every other body is a dwarf.

So Hazlitt metamorphoses the gallant Blücher (whom even Napoleon could afford to call an 'invincible old devil') into a 'wary adventurer;' and the generous ardour of the 'lyre and sword' young soldiers of Prussia into a 'brain-sick, pseudo-patriotism.' We were astonished to meet with such expressions, even in Hazlitt's Life of Napoleon. We hope we shall never be so unlucky as to stumble upon anything of the kind elsewhere. The man who can sympathize with the gospel of liberty in France only, and that gospel preached by NAPOLEON, has no heart to understand, consequently no pen to write, history.

But there is another false view of German patriotism which we are compelled to notice. Mr. Alison, in his great historical work (vol. vii.), eulogizing, as well he might, the noble stand which Austria, single-handed, made against Napoleon, in the campaign of 1809, finds the whole philosophy of this fact in the stability of aristocratic Governments. Aristocratic governments possess an element of stability, no doubt, which does not belong to the seething restlessness of pure democracy; but whether this element manifests itself in the persistence of a soulless tradition, or the inheritance of a lofty patriotism, is a matter that depends always on the quality of the aristocrats, which, as human affairs go, is as likely to be bad as good. As for

Austria, we think it was not Metternich, but the free mountain air, that inspired Hofer; and to have the steeple of St. Stephen's, and the coffee-houses of the Prater, besides fathers, and mothers, and brothers, and sisters before their eyes, was surely motive enough (without calling in the miracle of aristocracy) for the Austrians to drive Napoleon into the Danube at Aspern, and to make Macdonald pay sharply for his Marshal's baton at Wagram. The serfs of a despotic Government have a fatherland, on vital occasions, as much as the citizens of a free nation. Ride them on the back, and they will kick: bravely done; but it had been more brave, if they had never allowed the rider to get on.

Here indeed lies the mystery. How did it happen that France over-rode Austria so bravely from Jemappes to the battle of Leipzig, and paralysed Prussia, in 1806, by a single stroke, as if her very touch had been electricity? Was it the genius of the *redingote gris*, and the three-cornered hat, and the olive-complexioned face, and the eye, (what an eye!) and the mouth that could smile how kindly, and how deceitfully, that conquered Germany; or was it that certainly in part, but something else also? We think it was something else also, and mainly. Napoleon was the incarnated Siva of victory. This cannot be denied. But the assiduous plying of multitudinous cannon, despite of all tactical superiority, beat him back into Leipzig, and over the Rhine in 1813; why did it not do so in 1806? Not because the gunpowder was not there, but because there was no SOUL OF A GERMAN PEOPLE there to serve the guns, because Germany was beridden by aristocracy; that aristocracy being a mere gilded outside, prankt with all manner of vain gaudery; hence there was no independence, no freedom in Germany; no thoughts, no words, no SONGS of freemen, which are the alone proper fathers of heroic deeds. But in 1813 the tables were turned. It was good for aristocratic Prussia that she had been afflicted. In the hour of need (a cheap piety), Majesty falls suppliant to the supreme god—the People.[1] In the consciousness of omnipotence, the People lift Majesty out of the bog, generously bear him on their shoulders, and transport him, with whoop, and halloo, and patriotic jubilee, to Paris. Majesty responds eagerly to the popular cry. Majesty did not then profess to fight for 'legimacy,' as Talleyrand afterwards phrased it. Majesty was fighting for the liberty and independence of all

---

[1] The King, whose courage and prudence shone forth in a manner worthy of the descendant of the great Frederick, had been rescued, by the affectionate loyalty of his PEOPLE and ARMY, from the thraldom prepared for him.—Marquis of Londonderry's *War in Germany*, p. 13.

European peoples. Even about freedom of the press and representative constitutions, mystical words were thrown out—intended to remain mystical. Absolutism sailed over Europe, floated upon a sea of democracy. Strange phenomenon! and yet true; recorded in many histories and chronicles of bloody battles, found in many voluminous archives of state protocols and proclamations, and eternized also to our taste more pleasantly in many songs of the German fatherland, composed and sung by jovial Burschen, of whom every one could say, while he sung triumphantly—ET QUORUM PARS MAGNA FUI !

The Reformation in France, we read, was fanned by Marot's *chansons;* and Martin Luther in Germany combated the Devil very valiantly with an inkhorn (as the people in Eisenach show you), but more valiantly also, as he himself has left on record, by divine song. Had there not been music in Luther's soul, the Reformation—for a year and a day at least—might have gone back; for, in the hard conflict with that perfect impersonation of consistent Toryism, the Roman Pope, he required a comforter and familiar spirit to mellow him back to healthy humanity, after bathing in the theological vinegar of those days; and we know that he kept a sweet-singing bird in the inner chamber of his soul, more serviceable to those good Christians who know how

Songs of the Liberation War.

to value it, than any heathen δαίμων ever was to Socrates. Blessed be thou, Germany, fatherland of song! for Napoleon also, the invincible Cæsar, and the stern bridge-destroying Davoust, and Vandamme the 'blood-hound,' mob-hooted into Siberia, were conquered by the power of SONGS, whose name was LEGION. The songs of the German Liberation War were the utterance of a soul instinct with fire far fiercer than the cannon's. There are who delight to contrast poetry and fact. Shallow! All history that is worth reading is written in poetry; and he who does not write it poetically does not write it truly. The historian is merely a more modern name for the Epopoeist. If he cannot make an epos of the stuff before him, he has mistaken his subject or cannot handle his pen. He who sits down, with a most perverse erudition, to write a history of political bandboxes, and recite, most solemnly (like the Marquis of Londonderry in his *Tour in the North*), how many times the ladies of the Czarina change their dress in a day, proves his own relationship to the theme which he handles, not the barrenness of the luxuriant world in matters more pertinent. There is no lack of genuine epos—of great and good men, and great and good actions—in that much abused thing called modern history; for, despite of the vain pompous parading in court-dresses; despite the many-folioed accumulation of protocols, proclamations, despatches, reports, and what not, the mere mappery and paper projection of what has had, or may have, some relation to a deed; despite of espionage and 'necessary corruption' (as Frederick the Great would have it), intrigue, management, finesse, ruse, and the whole mysterious diplomatic craft of using words adroitly for the purpose of expressing what men do *not* mean to say; despite of all this lacing up of the soul scientifically, with the packthread of political deceit; despite of all these odious appurtenances, belonging, as we are told by some, without remedy, to the 'dignity' of modern history,—men, greatly honest, will still live and act truly in the world—honest hearts will sing out their honest faith, their triumphant conviction;

'For the soul triumphs with itself in words.'

And wherever these things are, in ancient or in modern times, you have poetry and reality in one—epos or ode, we care not which, sung or written, it does not affect the substance. Carlyle has written a glorious epos on the French Revolution. Of the Liberation War also an epos may be written, with fewer sublime horrors, indeed, of a Dantesque Hell to paint, but with more of the sacred flame from heaven to inspire. But hitherto the poetry of the

Liberation War has been principally developed in the lyrical shape., We have a broad billowy sea of national songs before us ; too loud and strong, too lusty and vigorous, perhaps, to be welcomed by all who delight in the atmosphere of effeminate artificiality which envelops our fashionable saloons ; but not the less true, not the less substantial, not the less precious to any man with whom poetry is something more than the lace on a lady's gown, and divine music a thing more serious than the wanton play of arabesques curiously tickling the ear-chambers of a fool. Blessed be God ! for a sturdy poetic swimmer in these piping times there is still one masculine enjoyment left—plunging with a full, fearless, outspreading of the whole man into the broad, strong-surging ocean of national song. There we make a dash to-day, into the bracing war-element of a substantial, *bona fide*, hard-fought battle, for the first right of man and the last—INDEPENDENCE. We hope many brave hearts are ready to join us. So pleasurable, indeed, is the fight of liberty to a generous mind, that if the old devil of despotism were killed outright to-day, one might almost wish him to come alive again to-morrow, that we might enjoy the triumph of conquering him a second time. And it is certainly not the most unphilosophical explication of the origin of evil, to say that vice exists only that virtue may have something to do; misery, to give benevolent men the pleasure of creating happiness; despotism, that there may be patriotism; a French Napoleon, that there may be a Liberation War in Germany; a feeble Government of paper and red-tape, that there may be a strong government by the brawn of a man's arm, and the mellow roar of an honest heart; Haugwitz, that there may be Hardenberg; Brunswick,[1] that there may be Blücher.

On the 17th day of March 1813—next after 1789, the most eventful year in recent history—the King of Prussia declared war against France. The proclamation which he issued to his people on that occasion brings vividly before us the cause and character of the great national struggle which followed; a sort of royal *imprimatur*, as it were, to that Bible of patriotic songs, in which the history of the time is written. It may be serviceable to translate it:—

---

[1] Not the hero of Quatre Bras, of course, but the Manifesto-maker of 1792, and the prating old man (nothing like Blücher) who held councils of war when he should have been fighting at Jena. ' *Ils se tromperont furieusement ces perruques!* ' said Napoleon in 1806 before that famous blow; and they did deceive themselves furiously indeed, even as much as the Emigrants, who sent multitudinous blusters into France in 1792, but were singularly weak and ineffective in their blows.

Songs of the Liberation War.

'TO MY PEOPLE.

' For my true people, and for all Germans, there is no necessity of a formal exposition of the causes of the present war: they lie bare to the eyes of Europe.

'We lay prostrate beneath the superior power of France. The peace which robbed me of one-half of my subjects, brought with it no blessings to compensate for so great a loss. Its wounds were deeper than those of the war. The marrow of the land was dried up; the principal fortresses remained in the possession of the enemy; agriculture was lamed; the industry of our cities paralysed. The freedom of trade was annihilated, and thereby the fountain of our prosperity sealed. The whole land was in a state of pauperism.

' By the most conscientious discharge of my obligations, I endeavoured to convince the French Emperor that it was his interest, as well as mine, to let Prussia resume her independence. But my sincerest attempts in the way of conciliation were nullified by arrogance and faithlessness; and we saw now, too plainly, that the Emperor's treaties, even more surely than his wars, aimed at our complete annihilation. The moment is now arrived when all illusions as to our real condition must cease.

' Brandenburgers, Prussians, Silesians, Pomeranians,

Lithuanians! you know what you have suffered for the last seven years.¹ You know what gloomy prospects are yours, if the struggle which we now begin be not gloriously ended. Think on your ancestors; think on the great Elector,² the great Frederick; think on the blessings which you enjoy as the fruits of what the swords of our ancestors gained under his captainship—freedom of conscience, honour, independence, commerce, manufactures, science. Think on the noble example of our powerful allies, the Russians; think on the Spaniards, of the Portuguese. Nations, less numerous than we, have marched into the field against a superior army, and have come off victorious. Think of the Swiss; think of the States.

'Great sacrifices will be demanded of all classes; for the struggle is great, and not small are the resources of our foe. You will be more ready to

---

[1] Davoust's cruelties in Hamburg, and the tender mercies of Vandamme in Bremen, were famous over all Europe. To all the supplications of the poor Hanseatists, the stern bridge-destroyer coolly replied—' *Vous n'avez rien en propre rebelles que vous êtes! votre peau même appartient à l'Empereur!*'—*Sketches of Germany and the Germans, by an Englishman* (London, 1836).

[2] Frederick William the Great, who kept France in check, and beat the Swedes at Fehrbellin in 1675. From this name the *modern* history of Prussia, so far as important European interests are concerned, may be dated.

make these sacrifices for your fatherland and for your own king, than for a foreign governor, who, as so much sad experience has taught, offers your sons and substance up as victims upon altars where the worship is not yours. Trust in God, perseverance, courage, and the powerful assistance of our allies, will crown our efforts with certain success.

'But whatever sacrifices we may be called upon to make, they are nothing when set in the balance against the holy rights for which we must contend; unless, indeed, we shall cease to be Prussians and Germans even in name.

'It is the last decisive struggle that we maintain for our wellbeing, our independence, our existence. There is no choice; between an honourable peace or a glorious destruction there is no medium. But even destruction you will face cheerfully for the sake of honour; for without honour a Prussian and a German will not live. But we have cause to hope with confidence, that God and our good-will will secure our just cause the victory; and with victory a glorious peace and the return of our national prosperity.

'FREDERICK WILLIAM.[1]

'BRESLAU, 17th March 1813.'

---

[1] *Geschichte des Deutschen Freiheitskrieges, vom* 1813 15, von Dr. Frederick Richter (Berlin, 1838), vol. i. p. 49.

Songs of the Liberation War.

This is a king's speech worth reading. There is honesty and pith in it; and, what is still more wonderful in royal orations, it strikes the very chord of popular opinion, and opens the gushing rivers of national poetry. But Necessity, that mighty mother (not of the world, as Shelley will have it, but of many things in the world), has done greater wonders than this: making absolute monarchs to understand (for a season) the genuine democratic principle of governing by public opinion. How the people replied to these noble words by nobler we shall hear anon in our songs; how they replied by deeds, the following extract, from the historical work just quoted, will best inform us :—

'From this moment the preparations for war were carried on with unexampled energy and enthusiasm. Thousands hastened from the workshops, from the comptoirs, from the halls of justice; the whole College of Government, at Breslau, offered itself to the King for the war service; but the King, honouring, as he could not but do, the spirit that animated these individuals, caused the Chancellor to issue a proclamation, prohibiting the public officers, in any of the great departments of State, from joining themselves to any volunteer Jäger corps.

'The universities and the upper classes of the gymnasia dissolved themselves by instinctive consent;

and the teachers were often the first to set the students an example of patriotic devotion to the national cause.[1] In vain was all protest on the part of the French Ambassador and the Commander of the French army in the Mark. All who were capable of bearing arms came thronging over the Oder, directing themselves either to Silesia or Colberg, where they were mustered and put under arms.

'The enthusiasm, indeed, went so far, that even women and maidens, giving the lie to their sex, went out and shared the hardest service with the men. Everything lived and worked only for war. The long restrained voice of indignation with which the Prussian people had for seven years borne the loss of liberty and honour, now burst into a flame; but honest love for king and country, and a faith not to be shaken in the Divine aid, elevated the strong motives of revenge to the noblest feelings of duty,

---

[1] Among the Gymnasiarchs, *Jahn* and *Steffens* boast the greatest celebrity (Varnhagen, v. 113). They were both in Lützow's volunteer corps, with Körner. Jahn was a most original character; a very apostle of 'Deutschthum' and nationality; a patriarch and prophet of the Liberation War. Men of this description were very serviceable to the King of Prussia before the battles were fought: they were the very soul by which he gained his victories. After the peace they were looked on as madmen, and treated as traitors. Not a few of them saw the inside of Spandau.

and to the firm determination to regain their lost character by the surrender of everything that they held dearest and best in life. To attain this end, no sacrifice was esteemed too great. Those who could not personally join in the great struggle gave, the poorest, his mite in the shape of contributions for the outfit of volunteers. The farmer, in many cases, gave up his last horse, that his only son might ride into the battle against the oppressor of his fatherland. Women brought their jewels, children and beggars their spare pennies, to the national purse. In Silesia, a young girl, with a beautiful growth of hair, sold it for two dollars, and sent the money to swell the national fund. In Berlin, under the direction of the Princess Wilhelm, the ladies formed themselves into societies for the tending of the wounded and others, who should suffer by the calamities of war. This good example was immediately followed almost in every city and town of the monarchy. Every family and social circle became a furnishing establishment for the great national arsenal; the iron work of the men, and the most slim fabrics of female skilfulness, were applied equally to the one great purpose. The very children in the schools occupied the vacation, and the hours of relaxation, in making *charpie* for the wounds; and little boys, spelling Nepos, ran after the army, with tears in their eyes, impatient now, at length, to be the heroes of whom they had so often read.'[1]

Such was the practical poetry of the Prussians in 1813; and if men, whose every word was at the same time a deed (as all true words ought to be), flung stirring songs, by the hundred, out of their honest German breasts, instead of twirling pretty verses upon their finger ends, as had been done by nice punctilious rhymers in more quiet times, Goethe's aristocratic nerves might be a little shaken in his artistical chamber; but poetry was poetry still, and strength was strength, and reality more powerful than fiction. Nay, and if here and there, and in all directions, the generous enthusiasm of regenerated nationality seemed to run wild in a real 'Berserker rage' of unchastened bellicosity—the madness of old Teutonic valour, that threw itself naked upon the sword of a foe, with a hurrah!—were not the French mad, too, with the old wine of the Revolution in their veins?—and was not Napoleon a very ΔΑΙΜΩΝ of battle, who could only be opposed by a power as transcendental as himself? 'May God fill you with hatred to the Pope!' said Martin Luther to his friends, when he left Smalkald. 'May God fill you with hatred to the French!' was what the Prussians

---

[1] Richter, p. 53; and *Narrative of an Eye-Witness in Odeleben's Saxon Campaign*, vol. ii. p. 114.

read in every motion, in every look of gallant old Blücher; and it was this spirit of thorough-going Germanism that made the veteran of the Katzbach to Napoleon the most obstinate 'Old Devil' that he ever had to contend with, and to the Germans the very Achilles and impersonated ideal of the war-epos of an age when every poet (except Goethe) was a soldier, and every soldier, by virtue of his cause, was a poet.

The patriotism of the Prussians broke forth with the greater might on this occasion, because it was a *smothered* flame. Not all the Prussians, perhaps not the majority, approved of the timid policy of the monarch in 1809. There was, and from 1806 had been, in the north of Germany a strong war-party, who could not be at all times as easily silenced as the Countess de Voss's parrot. The whole country was in a dark ferment of slow-gathering revenge. Napoleon might gag the tongues of men and birds, but he could not prevent the formation of secret societies and 'leagues of virtue,' where the seed was sown in the hearts of thousands, that merely waited for a word to start up into a host of armed men invincible. In connection with the *Tugendbund* or 'league of virtue' we make the following extract from Menzel:—

'The Tugendbund owed its existence to the Minister von Stein; but he having committed himself by a letter, the King, to please Napoleon, was obliged to dismiss him. Hardenberg, however, who succeeded to the office, was animated by the same spirit. The Tugendbund flourished in secret, numbering among its members many of the greatest statesmen, officers, and literati of the day. Among these latter, the two most distinguished were Arndt, by his power as a popular writer, and Jahn, by his influence as a trainer of youth. This man introduced the long-neglected gymnastic exercises into the curriculum of juvenile education; knowing well that weak and brawnless bodies are never without a fatal reaction on the moral qualities of the mind. He used to walk with his tiros under the Linden in Berlin, and, when they came to the Brandenburger gate, he used to say to each freshman—

' " Well, my lad, what are you thinking on now ?" and if the boy was stupid enough not to give a ready answer, he gave him a box on the ear, adding—

' " What should you be thinking on here but this, how the four horses that once stood on that gate, and were taken to Paris by the French, may be brought back here again, and placed where they were ?"'[1]

---

[1] Menzel's *Geschichte der Deutschen*, cap. 469.

A course of most instructive articles might be written on the regenerative process which Prussia went through, from the Battle of Jena to the Declaration of War in 1813; but we are no further concerned with the matter at present than to show, as briefly as possible, the soul out of which the patriotic and warlike melodies arose. We cannot, therefore, afford to enter into that most interesting history of RADICAL REFORMS, which preceded the great national uprising; but one short and tragic story in the previous history, an ominous flash of the slumbering volcano, is too closely interwoven with the living facts of patriotic poetry to be passed over in silence. We allude to the story of Schill. The English reader will find it at considerable length in the seventh volume of Mr. Alison. We take the following short notice from Menzel (c. 470 and 476), which extract, with Arndt's ballad, the words and music of which we have given below, No. I., will, we hope, be sufficient to command the sympathies of the reader.

'Austria, in the gallant stand she made for German liberty in 1809, was deceived in more points than one. She deceived herself in her own *Landwehr* (militia), numerous indeed and valiant; but *wanting that which alone can make a true soldier, the feeling of personal worth; subject to be flogged like serfs.* No less was Austria deceived in respect of Germany. Prussia was as yet too weak; all her fortresses in the hands of the French, and the new-born confidence in her old enemy Austria as yet not confirmed; and the members of the Rhenish confederation were still base enough to enjoy self-aggrandizement at the expense of Austria, even though they had to pay for this paltry gain with the loss of German independence, and servile submission to a man who was invincible so long only as German princes could not vanquish their selfishness.

'We must not suppose, however, that because Prussia could not afford formally to declare war against France in 1809, the hearts of the Prussians were therefore cold to the sacred cause. Many hearts burned in secret. The fiery Schill could not contain his enthusiasm, and rode at his own charge with a regiment of hussars from Berlin, amid general applause, though a decree of a court-martial immediately condemned his conduct. At the same time Dornberg rose in Hessia; and the plan was to raise the whole north of Germany. But Schill committed the fatal error of marching right north; and having thus separated himself from the Hessian and Westphalian patriots, he fell into the hands of the Danes, whose general, Ewald, without any order to that effect, out of sheer servility joined himself to the

Dutch, and, with an overwhelming number, shut up the rash hero in Stralsund. Schill fell in a bloody battle in the streets of that place, true to his own maxim—BESSER EIN ENDE MIT SCHRECKEN, ALS EIN SCHRECKEN OHNE ENDE.[1]

'The Dutch cut off his head, put it into spirit of wine, and exhibited it publicly in the University of Leyden, where it was still seen a few years ago. Nobody claimed it. But herein lies the grand beauty of the German heroes of those days, of Schill, Hofer, Speckbacher—they fought without a fee."[2]

The ballad which follows is a simple historical narrative in the old style, without any attempt at poetical adornment. Arndt was not an elegant and finished poet like Körner. He spoke to the people in the most common phrase of the people. So much the better; for the romances of real life which he sings are beauties that require no paint.

---

[1] Better an end with terror, than terror without an end.
[2] In the year 1835, the inhabitants of Stralsund erected a stone to the memory of Schill; and, about the same time, a monument was erected in Brunswick to twenty-five of Schill's officers, fourteen of whom had been shot in that town, and eleven in Wesel. Schill's head was redeemed by the Dutch, and laid to rest with the bones of the companions in arms of this distinguished German patriot.—DR. KOMBST.

Songs of the Liberation War.

ES ZOG AUS BERLIN EIN MUTHIGER HELD.
Melody I.

THE BRAVE SCHILL.

There went from Berlin a soldier stout, Juchhe !
Six hundred Ritter with him went out, Juchhe !
Six hundred Ritter all German and good,
And thirsting all for the Frantzmann's blood.
     Juchhe ! Juchhe ! Juchhee !
    O Schill, thy sabre smites sore !

He rode along in gallant trim, Juchhe !
And a hundred footmen marched with him, Juchhe !
God bless your guns, brave footmen all,
And with every shot may a Frantzmann fall !
    Juchhe, etc.

So marched the gallant stout-hearted Schill, Juchhe !
The Frantzmann, where he may come, shall feel, Juchhe !
No warrior, no king gave him command—
He was sent by freedom, by fatherland !
    Juchhe, etc.

At Dodendorf fatly the sandy soil, Juchhe !
Was fed with the blood of the Frantzmann vile, Juchhe !
Ten thousand that stood were hacked and hewed,
The remnant fled where the brave pursued.
    Juchhe, etc.

At Dömitz they stormed each strong redoubt, Juchhe !
And drove the villanous Frantzmann out, Juchhe !
To Pommerland now they come, they come,
And the Frantzmann's keen *qui vive* is dumb.
    Juchhe, etc.

Now bravely to Stralsund they ride, they ride, Juchhe !
'Like the billowy swell of the Baltic tide, Juchhe !
O Frantzmann, Frantzmann ! God lend thee wings !
'Tis Schill ! 'tis Schill ! and death he brings !
    Juchhe, etc.

Songs of the Liberation War. 27

Like thunder they tramp through the ancient town,
    Juchhe !
Which saw, without flinching, dark Wallenstein's frown,
    Juchhe !
Which sheltered the travel-worn Charles from the foe ;
O how are thy walls now, proud Stralsund, laid low !
      Juchhe, etc.

God save ye now, Frantzmenn ! the sword of the free,
    Juchhe !
For blood of the tyrant thirsts eagerly, Juchhe !
With blood of the Frantzmann gallantly gored,
Is brandished in triumph the German sword.
      Juchhe, etc.

O Schill ! O Schill ! thou soldier stout, O, weh !
They have hedged and snared thee round about, O, weh !
Many come from the land, and his coils from the sea,
The Dane, the snake, hath gathered for thee !
      O, weh ! O, weh ! O, weh !
      O Schill, thy sabre smote sore !

O Schill ! O Schill ! thou soldier stout, O, weh !
O, why wilt thou not to the fields ride out ? O, weh !
Shall walls imprison a heart so brave ?
In Stralsund shalt thou find thy grave ?
      O, weh ! etc.

O Stralsund, a sorrowful city art thou ! O, weh !
A sorrowful sight thou lookest on now ! O, weh !

Through the heart of the gallant the death-shot came ;
The base with the noble make pitiless game.
    O, weh ! etc.

A Frantzmann cried, with a butcher-cry, O, weh !
' The death of a dog the dog shall die !' O, weh !
May rooks and ravens batten on him,
Like a thief that dies on the gallows grim !
    O, weh ! etc.

They carried him forth, and all are dumb ; O, weh !
No fife to play ; no beat of the drum ; O, weh !
No cannon salute ; no greet of the gun,
To tell that the race of a soldier was run.
    O, weh ! etc.

With cruel sword they severed his head ; O, weh !
In an honourless pit his body they laid ; O, weh !
And there he sleeps, in the cool, cool grave,
Till God to honour shall wake the brave !
    Juchhe ! Juchhe ! Juchhe !
    O Schill, thy sabre smote sore !

In this translation we have thought it our duty to give the whole local details of the story, which the historian, and those intimately acquainted with the geography of Schill's march, would not willingly see omitted ; but those who wish to make this song *tell*, will confine themselves to Stralsund, omitting verses 2, 4, and 5. It is needless to say, that the sudden change from cheerful to sad, which takes place in the course of this ballad, affords a fine opportunity for a display of feeling and dramatic power on the part of the singer.

Our readers will have seen from the slight historical glance we have been able to cast, that, as the prostration of Germany proceeded from its division, so its rise was essentially connected with at least a temporary UNITY. Many dreamed in those days of Henry the Hun-hunter, Barbarossa, and the Hohenstauffen; political Puseyites, stamping reality with their pleasant whim: but a unity of soul for a great patriotic occasion, though not for permanent political action, was possible; even this, however, took place only partially. Mecklenburg, among German states, claims the high honour of having been the first to welcome Tettenborn and his Cossacks in the north; but Saxony, as is well known, the heart and centre of Deutschland, remained constant to Napoleon through the whole war, thus planting the strong nimble Frenchman in a position at Dresden, whence, as the Marquis of Londonderry very well expresses it, like a snake, 'he could twist and turn himself every way.' Bavaria also remained French during the greater part of the war. How much need, therefore, was there that, in the beginning of the year 1813, Arndt should send forth the famous song of the German's fatherland, which follows :—

WAS IST DES DEUTSCHEN VATERLAND?

Songs of the Liberation War.

WHERE is the German's fatherland?
The Prussian land? the Swabian land?
Where Rhine the vine-clad mountain laves?
Where skims the gull the Baltic waves?
    O no! O no! O no! O no!
    He owns a wider fatherland.

Where is the German's fatherland?
Bavarian land? or Styrian land?
Where sturdy peasants plough the plain?
Where mountain-sons bright metal gain?
    O no! etc.

Where is the German's fatherland?
The Saxon hills? the Zuyder strand?
Where sweep wild winds the sandy shores?
Where loud the rolling Danube roars?
    O no! etc.

Where is the German's fatherland?
Then name, then name the mighty land!
The Austrian land in fight renowned?
The Kaiser's land with honours crowned?
    O no! O no! O no! O no!
    'Tis not the German's fatherland.

Where is the German's fatherland?
Then name, then name the mighty land!
The land of Hofer?—land of Tell?
This land I know, and love it well;
    But no! etc.

Where is the German's fatherland?
Is his the pieced and parcelled land
Where pirate-princes rule? A gem
Torn from the empire's diadem?
    O no! O no! O no! O no!
    Such is no German's fatherland.

Where is the German's fatherland?
Then name, oh, name the mighty land!
Where'er is heard the German tongue,
And German hymns to God are sung!
    This is the land, thy Hermann's land;
    This, German, is thy fatherland.

This is the German's fatherland,
Where faith is in the plighted hand,
Where truth lives in each eye of blue,
And every heart is staunch and true:
    This is the land, the honest land,
    The honest German's fatherland.

This is the German's fatherland,
Which scorns the stranger's proud command;
Whose friend is every good and brave,
Whose foe is every traitor knave:
    This is the land, the one true land,
    The German's one true fatherland.

This is the land, the one true land,
O God, to aid be thou at hand!

And fire each heart, and nerve each arm,
To shield our German homes from harm,
To shield the land, the one true land,
One Deutschland and one fatherland.

We now plunge *in medias res* of the campaign with Marshal Blücher's March, a war-song full of fire, vigour, and truth, in which the 'hero of the Germans, the old man with a young heart,'[1] is enshrined in hallowing poetry, to live, we hope, as long as those of whom it was and is sung—

Ἐν μύρτου κλαδὶ τὸ ξίφος φορήσω.

Blücher, indeed, as we said before, is the real Achilles of this war; and, while our musical readers are educating their ear to the spirited air, No. III., which they will find a few pages on, we must endeavour to make a somewhat more intimate acquaintance with the hero of it, and pass shortly in review those glorious victories with which his name is so honourably connected.

Blücher was born in the year 1742 at Rostock, in Swedish Pomerania. In the year 1757 he entered the Swedish Hussars; and, in the year 1760, the Prussian service of Black Hussars; so that we find him, with the first down on his cheeks, in the same

---

[1] Der Held der Deutschen, der Greis mit dem Jünglingssinn.
—HEEREN.

character in which he appears in Arndt's celebrated song—

'*Was blasen die Trompeten?* HUSAREN *heraus!*'

By this reckoning we shall find that he was seventy-one years of age when he performed his valorous feats in the campaign of 1813; and some wise heads among those who arranged the plan of operations were certainly not *presumptively* to blame when they objected to Blücher that he was too OLD to do any good. But these did not *know* the man. There was more fire and genuine soldatesque Burschicosity about this old cavalry officer than in any mad French conscript that ever charged under the magic of Napoleon's personal command. Some objected, however, also to this. Blücher was too fiery, too impetuous, too headlong, as if the French had not won all their victories[1] by impetuosity, by their legs as much as their arms,[2] by their arms as much as by their heads. Blücher was, in fact, the very proper man to set against the French, accustomed to drive everything before them, and mistaking their mere celerity for superior ability. These conquerors of Europe, as they would then call themselves, looked upon the

---

[1] Bade, Nap. in 1813, ii. 136.
[2] The little corporal has discovered a new method of making war—he makes more use of our legs than our bayonets.—ALISON, v. 41.

Songs of the Liberation War. 35

Germans, *en masse*, as stupid, because they were slow. Once disabused of this conceit, their plumes quickly fell. Now, neither the Russians nor the Austrians could have struck, because they were not inclined to strike, such bold decisive blows as the fiery old hussar. The war was properly, indeed, a Prussian war; and if Kutusoff, and a strong party with him, thought they had done enough by pursuing Napoleon into Lusatia, it is easier to say that their soldiership was slack than that their wisdom was scant. But the watchword of Blücher and of the Prussians was 'FORWARDS!'—a word the soul of which must live in all great designs, but especially in all soldiership that shall merit the name. Blücher does not appear to have been a very learned tactician; in matters of science he trusted to Scharnhorst, and (when that great man fell at Lützen) to Gneisenau and Müffling; but he had the instinct of conquering, the ardent desire to beat, and the dogged determination not to be beaten. When he headed the furious charge at the Katzbach, with his old grey hair streaming in the wind, and his drawn sword gleaming to the lightning of the furious tempest (for it was fearful weather), and the warm hearty cry from his German throat—'*Nun vorwärts, Kinder!*' in the living drama of this act lay a victory such as no learning of Barclay de Tolly, or prudence of Langeron, could have gained; and the fact was, that the very parties who distrusted him at first, now saw that they could have done nothing without him. The Russians hailed him with three cheers as the 'Archangel Michael,' or what to them seemed a synonym for that, 'the little Suwarrow.' It was in vain now that each wise Ulysses of the allied army (and there were many—*too* many) might look down with learned complacency on the unscientific Blücher as the mere 'blockish Ajax' of battle. To his soldiers he was Achilles; and, if no Achilles, then the Liberation War had only an Ajax for its best soldier; and Ajax we shall be content to call him, less poetically perhaps, but more truly than the higher similitude; for it is not to be denied that there was something rude, rough, bearish, if you will, about this old hussar. He was a BURSCH, with all the vices and all the virtues of a Bursch—a Bursch with grey hairs too, given to dicing, and other military recreations; a gross offence in the eyes of many decent, smooth-faced, respectable people; but Nature, who does not always make saints valiant, sometimes makes valiant men little saintly. The French thought him very rude in Paris. He used to go and dine at the *restaurateurs'*, *en particulier*; and *sans cérémonie*, when the heat annoyed him, take off his coat, and fling it over the chair, 'to the great surprise of the garçons, *et aux applaudissements*

Songs of the Liberation War. 37

des Anglais, qui voyaient dans cette absence de toute gêne une certaine conformité avec leur humeur.[1] When young, he had been a famous duellist. He quarrelled with his superior officer about some practical joke he had played off upon a Polish priest; and Frederick the Great having been duly informed of the freak, refused him an expected promotion. Blücher, in dudgeon, left the army, carrying with him the old infidel's polite dismissal—'*Est congédié, et peut aller au diable*' (*kann sich zum Teufel scheeren!*) In all this we see signs of a temper tough even to obstinacy, independent even to rudeness; and we may well suppose that (before the battle of the Katzbach) Blücher was, as we are told, 'no great favourite at Court.' But the grand thing about him was his thorough Germanism; he was a '*Franzozenfresser*,' French-eater, of the genuine kind; and though he had served at Kunersdorff under French Fritz, he had picked up so little of the language of *Sans Souci* that, in the year 1813, after crossing the Elbe, and joining with Bernadotte, he could hold no communication with the dilly-dallying Crown Prince (whose heart naturally enough was not in Berlin, but in Stockholm) except by the aid of an interpreter. When the campaign of

---

[1] *Biographie Universelle.* Blücher *par Parisot.* Does this man imagine that we are all pugilists and jockeys?

1814 was successfully ended, he showed his true German spirit, in a somewhat wild way, by insisting that the bridge of Jena should be blown up, to annihilate for ever this witness of Prussian shame; and he was actually at the work, when the most high and mighty potentates of the north decently interfered and put a stop to this escapade of military Burschicosity. Thus, we perceive, as Shakespeare says of that same Ajax, that his valour was sometimes 'crushed into folly;' we hope we may say, also, that his folly was 'sauced with discretion.' He liked to act independently, indeed, as much as possible; he could only perform his '*Husarenstreiche*' (like that of *Haynau*) himself; but he was willing to take good advice when he could get it, and where he could plainly see that it was consistent with valour as much as with prudence. 'You will make me a *doctor*,' said he to the Oxford square-caps. 'You must then make my friend Gneisenau an *apothecary;* for I never do anything without him!' the speech of a good fellow, such as Blücher was; a man, take him all in all, worthy to stand on a pedestal beside the royal palace at Berlin, and to live for ever in the hearts of jovial Burschen, singing a song that shall be as immortal as Napoleon.

The course of the campaign of 1813, from the battle of Lützen to that of Leipzig, is pretty well indicated in the words of our song, p. 51 below. A few words of commentary, however, will be necessary. The campaign divides naturally into three parts : the forward movement of Napoleon from Leipzig to Breslau ; the armistice ; the renewal of hostilities, and the forward movement of the allies from Silesia, Bohemia, and Brandenburg to Leipzig, from Leipzig to the Rhine, and from the Rhine, by the campaign of 1814, finally to Paris. At the commencement of the war, the movements of both parties necessarily were *offensive;* on the part of Napoleon, that he, by striking a bold blow, with the least delay possible, might reinstate himself in his former position, and prove to sceptical Europe that the *snow* ONLY had driven him back from Moscow ; on the part of the Russo-Prussian allies that they might, by an energetic advance, rouse the heart of Germany, and break the bands of the Confederation of the Rhine. Hence the necessity of crossing the Elbe and entering Dresden, where the hearty shouts of '*Fort mit den Franzosen!*' which received them, proved that, if the People had been king, Saxony would have been German (and with it, perhaps, Bavaria and Württemberg), without the necessity of Leipzig. Both armies being thus determined on attack, the occasion could not be long wanting. Blücher in the van (as usual with him) attacked the French army when on the road from Weissenfels to Leipzig, near Lützen—the celebrated battle-field that saw Gustavus Adolphus, the hero of Protestantism, conquer and die. Napoleon was surprised; the French were, during the early part of the fight, driven back by the irresistible onset of Blücher with his Prussians (the old veteran himself was wounded, but never left the field), but Napoleon rallied; in the evening, his two wings, under Bertrand and Eugene, came up with fresh troops, and the lost ground was recovered. Night closed on the battle; and the Germans did *not* leave the field till next morning, when they commenced a retreat towards Silesia in the best possible order, and receiving not the least damage from Napoleon. The Emperor lost 10,000 men and the Germans as many. For these reasons they are naturally unwilling to say that Napoleon gained the battle; and in our song it is legitimately celebrated as one of Blücher's noblest exploits. But a retreat always looks like a defeat, whether made on the day of the battle, or on the morning immediately following; and, as it never can be made without leaving the pursuer the advantage of a certain quantity of ground, and all the advantages that flow from the possession of that ground, Napoleon, we must say, gained the battle of Lützen (2d May). He advanced to Leipzig, to Dresden; and to all public appearance Richard was himself

Songs of the Liberation War. 41

again. This was the main point gained. The allies, on the other hand, were forced to retreat into Silesia, leaving Hamburg and Halle (taken by Bülow) in the lurch; and the next blow that followed at Bautzen in Lusatia (21st May), in all material circumstances a mere repetition of the first, completed the ostensible superiority of Napoleon. There he was again, as if by magic, after total overthrow and utter prostration, in the course of a few months, at Leipzig, at Dresden, at Breslau, with his left hand greedy to grasp Berlin, in the fair way to deal with the Prussians as he had dealt with the Austrians in 1809, at Znaym. And, strange enough, here, too, an armistice followed, after two bloody battles, as in the other case; but what followed the armistice was altogether of a different complexion.

The armistice was concluded on the 4th June, and lasted till the 17th August. That it was concluded at all, proves how Napoleon had exhausted himself in the two great battles which had brought him from Leipzig to Breslau; he had now tested the temper of his foes; and if this spirit should continue, and prove infectious (as patriotism is apt), there was every danger to be apprehended. But the armistice came, and the danger with it; Napoleon trusting, as he had so often done, to the stupidity of his adversaries, and to his star. But the event deceived him. Wellington was thundering at the foot of the Pyrenees; and Metternich came to Dresden personally, and with the utmost coolness talked of dissolving the Confederation of the Rhine, and confining France within France. Napoleon was blank with astonishment; he fumed; he stamped; his hat fell on the ground; and Napoleon lifted it up himself. The issue of this is plain. The Austrians who, during the armistice, put themselves forward as mediators, ended with declaring themselves enemies. The war was renewed, on both sides, with united energy, and more desperate determination.

We do ourselves the pleasure here, before going further, to insert two poems, written during the armistice; one very flattering to us, hailing Wellington in his progress over the Pyrenees;[1] the other showing with what warm appeals the Prussian patriots invoked the powerful aid of Austria. The Prussians, in the excess of a just national pride, sometimes boast that *they* saved Europe in 1813. Had Austria then behaved as Prussia did in 1809, where had Prussia been now?

---

[1] Comp. Alison, ix. 356 and 424.

THE GERMANS TO WELLINGTON IN SPAIN.

(*Wellington defeated Soult, near Roncesvalles, on the 28th July* 1813.)

SING ye Old Roland's lay!
Sing routed France to-day!
Sing Roncesvalles!
See! from far seas appear,
Eager for blood the spear,
And its red gleam in fear
Scatters the Gaul!

Hail to thee, Wellington!
Glory's wreath thou hast won,
Bloody and red.
Where Roland fought of yore,
Rolled British cannon's roar,
And the proud Gaul in gore
Reeking is laid!

Hail to thee, gallant Lord,
Freedom's own shield and sword,
Helmet and spear!
Blood of the Percies now
Mantles the Briton's brow;
Horn of brave Roland, blow
Blasts of pale fear!

Where the bright orange blows,
Where the grape ruddy glows,
Rest in thy bays;

Thee the Moor's gates invite,
Welcome thee Lord and Knight,
Thee Spanish maidens bright
Gleefully praise!

Hail! to thee, happy isle,
Where freedom's blossoms smile
Bright in the main!
Fiery steeds prancing high,
Billows that flout the sky,
Arrows that cheat the eye,
Storm it in vain!

Lofty Britannia!
Hold thou the seas in awe,
Steady and sure!
Be thou strong Freedom's wall,
Let the wide welkin's hall
Echo back Roncesvalles
And Agincourt!

THE GERMANS TO THEIR EMPEROR.

July 1813.

GERMAN Kaiser! German Kaiser!
Come, our saviour, our avenger!
Save thy Deutschland from the stranger,
Take the wreath we wove for thee.

Songs of the Liberation War. 45

See the league is true and German!
Only German hopes have swayed us,
Only thou and God shall aid us,
Not the Dane, and not the Swede.

Come, in ancient holy harness!
See thy sires entreat, adjure thee!
Of Germania's weal secure thee,
Make the empire's freedom sure.

Like a shepherd, strong yet gentle,
Rudolph from his Alps descended,
Jarring strifes in peace were blended,
Under Habsburg's kindly sway.

Praise to thee, fleet Chamois-hunter!
War his tent, and her pavilion
Peace, for thee, brave Maximilian
Spreads—our Kaiser-Cavalier!

When dissension tore the empire,
Shaking ancient Faith's foundations,
Deutschland pined among the nations
Thirty dark and dreary years.

With no tears to spare for pity,
Half apostle, and half warrior,
'Gainst the storm a strong rock-barrier
Stood the pious Ferdinand.

German Kaiser! German Kaiser!
Lagg'st thou?—sleep'st thou?—up, awaken!

46 Songs of the Liberation War.

Let the lion's mane be shaken !
Be a Rudolph ! be a Charles !

Let the EMPIRE be the watchword !
Where the ancient banner leads us,
Where the eagle's pride precedes us,
We will march to victory.

Cast not off what God hath given !
On thy German throne reseated,
Kaiser crowned, and Kaiser greeted,
Be the star of Christendom ![1]

The armistice left Napoleon in possession of the whole line of the Elbe, with his head-quarters at Dresden. The plan of the allies was well conceived. They were composed of three great divisions—the Bohemian army under Schwartzenberg, the Silesian army under Blücher, the army of the north under Bernadotte and Bülow; *and* Bülow, we are obliged to say, because, though the Crown Prince, the only nominal commander, put on his military cloak, he behaved as if he had forgot to put a sword under it. With these three armies, and with the Polish reserve

---

[1] These poems are by Schenkendorf (*Werke*, Berlin, 1837), one of those amiable enthusiasts, whom we have already characterized as political Puseyites, fondly hoping that it might be as easy to bring in a German Emperor, in the nineteenth century, as to drive out a French one. The most of them, naturally enough, were also Romanists.

Songs of the Liberation War. 47

under Benningsen, the allies far outnumbered Napoleon; and their policy evidently was to give him smart blow after smart blow, whenever he should attempt, from his central situation, to send out rash feelers in this direction or in that; and after wounding him sorely, and making him draw back from all attempts at the offensive, hem him into some corner, and cannon him into the other world, or, at all events, out of Germany. And so they managed; admirably well in all things, except in the attack they made on Dresden, without (as the partial German historian himself confesses) exactly knowing what they were about; and, while they made a big blunder, thus giving Napoleon occasion to boast (as he always did) that he had gained a brilliant victory.[1] Despite of this, however, the plan succeeded. At Gross Beeren, on the 23d August, Oudinot, Napoleon's first feeler towards Berlin, was cut keenly by Bülow; on the 26th, his second towards Silesia, Marshal Macdonald, was crushed and utterly prostrated by Blücher in the brilliant victory of the Katzbach, which has been well termed the vanguard

---

[1] All parties agree that the attack on Dresden was a blunder, which might have proved fatal. Schwarzenberg explained it in an admirable way. '*There is no commanding,*' says he, '*with emperors and kings on the spot.*'—Marquis of Londonderry, p. 122.

of Leipzig. This blow was closely followed by the annihilation of Vandamme in the defiles of the Bohemian mountains, 30th August ; and, on the 6th September, Bülow (at Dennewitz), with that same Prussian pith which had conquered at the Katzbach, kept his ground for a whole day against Marshal Ney with overpowering numbers, till, in the evening, the Swedes and Russians came up to secure to him his well-won laurels. Then, with an alacrity which Napoleon (who thought no one had legs but himself) could not understand, the gallant old hero of the Katzbach—now reigning, by the magic of victory, over the hearts of a once divided army[1]—stole a march out of Silesia; and, in the face of very strong French fortifications, and on very disadvantageous ground, crossed the Elbe at Wartenburg (2d and 3d October), and united with the Crown Prince, who was advancing with the northern army over the same river by Dessau. Napoleon was thus being hemmed in, not only by superior numbers, but by soldiers whose inspired soldiership had driven the vain and mercenary French out of every post which they had attempted to hold. It was easy, indeed, to

---

[1] The Russians were somewhat offended, at first, at being put under a German. In the Bohemian army, Alexander also was piqued that he had not been made Generalissimo. The brave Cossacks certainly deserved more respect.

call the brilliant victories of Katzbach and Dennewitz the 'disasters of Marshals Ney, Oudinot, and Macdonald.' No man understood the art of newspaper-painting better than Napoleon; but the fact remained, that the French had been shamefully beaten once and again, *not* by superior numbers, but by superior soldiership; and here, as in all wars—

> ' Each success,
> Although particular, did give a scantling
> Of good or bad unto the general;
> And in such indexes—although small pricks
> To their subsequent volumes, there is seen
> The baby figure of the giant mass
> Of things to come at large.'

And so it proved. Napoleon retreated from Dresden (7th October), doggedly retracing the footsteps which he had tracked in so much blood. He posted himself with his back to Leipzig, his front facing the wider line of the allies in a convex semicircle towards the north, east, and south of the town; and there, after a stand of three days, and under a cannonade which made the earth literally tremble, he was obliged at last to yield to the overpowering united energy of determined enemies, whom he had made several desperate attempts to strike singly, but failed in all. Blücher was at Leipzig also; and by the eagerness (so unlike the slowness of the Austrian Archdukes in 1809) with which he struck home against Marmont on the first day, the 16th, contributed not a little to the utter rout and prostration which followed on the 18th and 19th, when the great Continental Colossus fell, limbless, never again to rise, except in fits and convulsions (as at Waterloo), like the memory of a hideous dream, making a man's blood freeze in broad daylight.

The course of Blücher's victories, as we have thus hastily run them over, is given in the words of the song which follows. But the Katzbach, with its 20,000 prisoners, 103 cannon, and 250 tumbrils claimed a separate poetical apotheosis. This it received from Follen, in a fierce-rushing style, suiting well both with the fierceness of the Prussian onset under Blücher, and the dark tempestuous weather, and opening of the flood-gates of heaven, with which it was accompanied. The words of this we subjoin to the song of Blücher. The billowy Trochaic rhythm of the original is strictly preserved; and those who can command two strong bass voices will find the music in Follen's *Harfen-grüsse aus Deutschland und der Schweitz*, Zürich, 1823.

Songs of the Liberation War.

WAS BLASEN DIE TROMPETEN.

March time. MELODY III.

Why blare loud the trumpets?—to horse, ye hussars!
'Tis the gallant old field-marshal that rides to the wars!
So cheerily rides he his own good steed,
So brightly his sword flashes time to his speed;
      Sound, etc.

O see how his blue eye, so clear and so kind,
Is beaming, and wave his white locks to the wind!
Like a stout old wine, so mellow and so fine,
O he's the man to marshal the sons of the Rhine!
      Sound, etc.

Songs of the Liberation War. 53

O he is the man, when all was dark and dim,
Who waved his sword in Heaven's eye—'twas all
    bright to him !
He swore by his true steel to teach them yet aright—
He swore an angry oath—how the Germans can fight.
    Sound, etc.

His good oath he kept : when the war-cry rang,
On his horse, with a bound, bold Blücher sprang ;
And his clear blue eye shot fire to wash the shame
Of Auerstadt and Jena from the German name.
    Sound, etc.

At Lützen, impatient, he headed the van,
Like a strong young lion, the old veteran :
There the Teut first taught the hot Frenchman to
    bleed,
By the altar of freedom, the stone of the Swede.[1]
    Sound, etc.

---

[1] 'Close by the road, at Lützen, is the spot where Gustavus fell under repeated wounds, buried beneath a heap of dead piled above his corpse, in the dreadful conflict which took place for his dead body. A number of unhewn stones, set horizontally in the earth, in the form of a cross, mark the spot. On one of them is rudely carved, in German—GUSTAVUS ADOLPHUS, KING OF SWEDEN, FELL HERE FOR LIBERTY OF CONSCIENCE. A shapeless mass that rises from the centre of the cross, and since that day has been called "The Stone of the Swede," bears merely the initials of the monarch's name. Though in a field, and close on the road, neither plough nor wheel has been allowed to profane the spot. Some pious hand has planted round it a few poplars, and disposed within the circle some rude

Songs of the Liberation War.

The Katzbach was red with the fierce drifting rain,
But eve saw it redder with the blood of the slain!
'Fare-thee-well, fare-thee-well! and fairly may'st thou sail,
And find a grave, false Frantzmann, with the Baltic whale.'
    Sound, etc.

Then forward, my brave boys, begun's half done:
We'll teach the nimble Corsican to run, boys, run!
O'er the Elbe, o'er the Elbe, now Preuss and Swede advance,
And the fleet Don Cossack with his long, long lance!
    Sound, etc.

On the red field of Leipzig he laid the French pride low;
He blew the blast of freedom loud at Leipzig, Oho!
They fell, there they fell, ne'er to rise from their fall;
And we cheered old Blücher there—Long live the Field-marshal!
    Sound, etc.

Then blow loud, ye trumpets, and tramp, ye hussars!
'Tis our old Field-marshal that rides to the wars:

---

benches of turf, where the wanderer may linger, musing on the deeds and the fate of a heroic and chivalrous monarch.'—Russell's *Tour in Germany*, i. 23. 'Some years ago a monumental arch was erected over this stone, and the spot laid out and adorned in a manner more worthy of the hero who fell there.'—DR. KOMBST.

To the Rhine, to the Rhine, and beyond the Rhine's
the way,
Thou doughty old Field-marshal, and God be with thee
aye!
  Sound, etc.

THE WAR-DANCE OF THE KATZBACH.

On the Katzbach, on the Katzbach,
There the strife was red and ruddy!
There we danced the fearful war-dance
With the Frantzmann base and bloody!

There an ancient German gleeman
Struck the strong bass deep and hollow;
Marshal Forwards,[1] Prince of Walstatt,
Leads, and where *he* leads we follow.

Fearful was the hall dark-vaulted
With the flashing flame of war lit;
Broad were spread the bright green carpets;
Blücher soon will dye them scarlet.

He hath played a boding prelude,
First at Goldberg, and at Jauer;
Now he comes, like gathered Boreas,
Organing with giant power.

---

[1] MARSHAL FORWARDS.—So Blücher was familiarly called by the soldiers, for reasons sufficiently obvious.

Ay ! it was no gentle tripping ;
'Twas a fierce and fitful battling,
Like the night-blast strong and startling,
In the wind-mill wheels loud rattling.

Who is this beside the gleeman,
On the big drum beating loudly,
Like the god that bears the hammer,
Through the battle walking proudly ?

Gneisenau, the staunch true Ritter !
Hero-pair, that pledged our speeding,
Deutschland's living double eagle;
Where they pounced, the prey lies bleeding !

And it swells more loud, more rapid !
Where the dance is wildest spinning,
Every Frantzmann seeks his fair one,
And he finds—a death-skull grinning.

Where the whirling waltz was hottest,
In the thickest sultry slaughter,
When both blood and brain were boiling,
He cooled you in the Katzbach's water.

Hear the river roaring vengeance—
' Sleep no more on stranger-pillows !
Ye have sucked the blood of Deutschland ;
I will suck you in my billows !'

Thus, with sabre sharp, bold Blücher,
In Death's dark books thou didst write them ;

Through the surly smoke of battle,
Like a war-god, thou didst smite them !

Thus 'twas fought by German people,
Not by bondmen, not by princes ;
God, to right the wrongs of ages,
Measures not revenge by inches.

' Blücher, Katzbach !' cry, O Prussia !
Thou who lay'st in sorest trouble ;
Gird thy loins with manhood doubly,
And thy glory shall be double.

' Blücher, Katzbach !' shout, ye Germans,
Where the goblet gaily glances,
Till our sires, with Hermann's chorus,
Answer from the hall of lances.

II.

A NICHE FOR KÖRNER.

> Ich war ein freier Jäger in Lützow's wilder Schaar,
> Und auch ein Zitterschläger, mein Schwertlied klang so klar;
> Nun reiten die Genossen allein auf ihrer Fahrt,
> Da ich vom Ross geschossen, und hier begraben ward.
> RUECKERT.

> A song for the death of the brave;
> A song of pride!
> The youth went down to a hero's grave,
> With the sword his bride!
> FELICIA HEMANS.

OUR gallant septuagenarian soldier-Bursch, Marshal Blücher, whose 'helmet pressed hoariness,' sleeps now on the roadside between Breslau and Schweidnitz, tented by the blue heavens and three solitary lime-trees. Beneath an oak at Wöbbelin (a mile from Ludwigslust in Mecklenburg) sleeps another hero of that heroic war; and the lyre and sword upon his tomb, symbols of Tyrtean glory, teach the passing traveller that here is the grave of Theodore Körner.

It is not our intention, on the present occasion, to say again what has been said about this gallant poet-soldier a hundred times. He was not a man of words. With him every word was either the prophet, or the accompaniment, or the memory, of a deed; and such words only have truth in them, and with truth immortality.

Those who wish to inform themselves about Körner, personally and poetically, can complain of no lack of English aids. Mr. Richardson, Mr. Chorley, and *Tait's Magazine*,[1] will gratify the most comprehensive curiosity. All that remains for us to do now is, to connect Körner with the general history of the Liberation War, given in our last chapter, and enable the lover of music to sing, with understanding, the celebrated "black troopers' chase," which appears first (No. IV.) in our present selection. We shall thus have given our readers as complete a historico-lyrical sketch of the famous Liberation War as our limits will admit. For something more detailed we think we may refer our readers with confidence to Alison's *History of Europe*, vol. ix.

The army of the Allies, in 1813, the reader will recollect, after the breaking up of the armistice (17th August), advanced against Napoleon in three directions: Schwartzenberg, with the kings and emperors, from Bohemia; Blücher from Silesia; and Bernadotte

---

[1] Vol. i. 732, first series; vol. i. 701, second series.

from Berlin. Covering Bernadotte's extreme right, over against Holstein, stood a corps of some 22,000 or 25,000 men, under a commander, whose full name, according to the self-comprehending German fashion, is written 'The Russian-Great-Britannical-Lieutenant-General-Von-Wallmoden-Gimborn.' Facing Wallmoden, on the French side, stood Davoust, leagued with the Danes; his headquarters Hamburg. A line drawn due south from Lübeck on the Baltic to Lauenburg on the Elbe, in its southern half almost identical with the course of the river Stecknitz, marks, nicely enough, the position of the two corps, the one eastward and the other westward, at the recommencement of the war. The advantage, in respect of number and organization, was altogether on the side of the French; and, so far as generalship was concerned, the young glowing heart of Körner, who served here, might beat with no ignoble expectation of fronting in fight the stern and taciturn tyrant of Hamburg, whose eyes looked mill-stones (as Shelley says that Lord Eldon wept them), and tearing the bloody laurels from the brow of the hero of Auerstädt, Eckmühl, and Wagram. But Davoust, whose hat had been struck off, and his coat literally riddled with ball, at Auerstädt, seemed, on the marshy banks of the Stecknitz, to have sunk into a total dullardness and stagnation of soul. His obstinacy, indeed, for which he was so famous, did not desert him; but its virtue, which the poor Hamburgers had so often felt to be positive, was here merely negative; he seemed obstinate only *not* to fight. Various conjectures have been made as to the cause of the Frenchman's backwardness on the present occasion. He had certainly no commands from Napoleon to that effect. An intercepted letter, on the contrary, shows that the Emperor wished him to assume boldly the offensive, and push ;on to Berlin.¹ Why, indeed, should he have delayed?—there was every reason for expedition. A single well-fought battle might have cleared the north of Germany of insurgents, hemmed in the rear of the Swedes, lent a right arm of strength to Oudinot at Gross Beeren and to Ney at Dennewitz, and driven the timid Crown Prince into Stralsund, there to look through the spy-glass of diplomatic possibilities anxiously towards Christiania and the Dovrefjeld mountains. Alison, in his history of the campaign of

---

¹ 'Je suppose qu'aujourd'hui (17th August) ou demain vous aurez attaqué ce qui est devant vous : si l'ennemi vous est inférieur en force, ne vous laissez pas masquer par un petit nombre et par une CANAILLE, telle que les Anséates, la légion (our German legion), et les troupes de Wallmoden. Il n'y a de bonnes troupes contre vous que les Suèdes, et à peu près le quart de ce qu'a Bülow, qui est troupe de ligne.'—NAPOLEON.—Beamish's *History of the King's German Legion*, vol. ii. p. 183.

Wagram, says the arrival of the Archduke John, from Pressburg, three hours sooner, would have saved Austria, roused Germany, and anticipated Leipzig by four years. We believe this—of such consequence is despatch in business; and we say, in like manner, that if Marshal Davoust, in the month of August 1813, with his 30,000 French and 10,000 Danes, instead of hiding himself, like a hermit,[1] amid the lakes, and marshes, and woods of Mecklenburg, had come out boldly as Germans were accustomed to see Frenchmen come, and struck home sternly as the Duke of Auerstädt might have been expected to strike, Gross Beeren and Dennewitz might have been converted into the preludes of some French Leipzig, and Marshal Ney made King of Berlin before the Bourbon saw Paris. But it is merely a *might*, a possibility, of course; and, at best, a matter of delay. For the soul of the German people was up; and, while Austria and Prussia held together, the show of French supremacy in Germany, for a few years longer, could only have been the pledge of a more terrible prostration.

As it was, however, Marshal Davoust did not advance; and the consequence was that he in Silesia, who was determined at all hazards to advance, Mar-

---

[1] *Hermite de Ratzebourg* was the nickname he got at this period.—*See* Von Ense's *Denkwürdigkeiten*, vol. iii. p. 452.

shal FORWARDS, was allowed to give a decided character to the whole war. After the glorious victory of the Katzbach, the French were forced to act throughout on the defensive. At Leipzig, the concentrated Allies girded them round with inevitable destruction; and Davoust stood cooped in at Hamburg, as useless, if not altogether as inglorious, as General Mack (in 1805) at Ulm.

Of Wallmoden's corps and Lützow's black troopers, one of its most remarkable component parts, we translate the following account from the German historian:—

'The corps was composed, indeed, of the most heterogeneous elements; but the majority were men of education and high respectability. The English, the Hanoverians, the Russo-German Legion, the Mecklenburgers, Dessauers, and Hanseatists, were mostly all volunteers; and many of them had drawn the sword for Germany and Europe at their own cost. The same may be said of the regiment of Cossacks commanded by the famous General Tettenborn. The Cossack, indeed, is never a soldier on compulsion. All these troops were animated with a spirit of courage and determination that might well compensate for lack of training and organization. The great aim of the struggle was here, if anywhere, recognised in all its importance; and the event showed how much the spirit of patriotism, in a truly popular war, is superior to the mechanics of soldiership.

'These remarks apply with peculiar force to Lützow's volunteer corps. The Cossacks called the Crown Prince of Sweden "The eye of the army"—rather a satirical sort of compliment, implying that the merit of the Swede did not lie in his *deeds*. But with the utmost truth we may say, that in Lützow's volunteer corps lived the *idea* of the war. The universal enthusiasm elevated itself here to a noble self-consciousness. In the other corps, this and that individual might attain the same high intellectual position that was the property here of the whole body; the soldier entered with full sympathy into the dignity each man of his personal mission, and fought from clear conviction, not from blind impulse. Those loose and roving adventurers that, to a certain extent, will always mix themselves up with a volunteer corps, were kept in check here by the number of high and noble spirits with whom they found themselves in daily communion. Here, whatsoever glowed with holy revenge against the recklessness of a foreign tyranny; whatsoever, in other parts of Europe, had manifested itself to be animated by a spirit of unyielding animosity to Napoleon's despotism; whosoever had learned, under long-conquering banners, to curse the conquests and to despise the conqueror,

A Niche for Körner. 65

were gathered together in one knot of many-coloured, but one-hearted fellowship. These men were all penetrated by the conviction that, in the nature of things, no power merely military, no cunning of the most refined despotism, can, in the long-run, triumph over native freedom of thought and tried force of will. They looked upon themselves as chosen instruments in the hand of the divine Nemesis, and bound themselves by a solemn oath to do or to die. They were in fact virtually free, when Germany yet lay in chains; and for them the name of "Free Corps" (*Frei-Schaar*) had a deeper significancy than that of free (volunteer) soldiers. Here the deed of the individual was heralded by the thought that measured inwardly, and rejoiced in the perception of its own capability. Here the triumphant spirit of patriotism broke forth in song, in poetry, which is the outspread wing of enthusiasm. The prince, the philosopher, the bard, served under Lützow, as volunteers, in the humblest capacity. The Prince of Karolath, Steffens, Jahn, Theodore Körner, and many other consecrated names, belonged to this noble body. Nay, even females, under well-concealed disguises, came boldly forward to share with this brave band all the toils and hardships of the sterner sex.[1] The enemies of France, from Spain

[1] The most remarkable of these Prussian heroines was Leo-

and the Tyrol, joined themselves to this corps, trusting to find here, at length, that revenge of their righteous cause which a mysterious Providence had hitherto delayed. Riedl and Ennemoser commanded a body of Tyrolese sharpshooters, and among them was the son of Andrew Hofer. From the French armies, Dutchmen and Saxons, Westphalians and Altmarkers,[1] rejoiced to belong to the "Black Corps" (*Die Schwarze Schaar*), as these troops, from their uniform, were familiarly named. In the whole body there was scarcely an individual who, on the

---

nora Prochaska, daughter of a music-master in Potsdam, who served in Lützow's corps disguised as a young man, under the name of Augustus Rentz. Her tall figure and noble bearing had preserved the secret of her sex. Her obliging manners, modesty, and good conduct, in every respect, had secured her the friendship of her fellow-soldiers and the esteem of her superiors. On the day of the 16th September, in the affair of Göhrdewalde, she was one of the first who rushed on the squares of the enemy, and was struck by a ball on the left thigh, which laid her on the ground. She now discovered herself to the officer who was engaged in procuring the assistance of a surgeon. The surgeon declared her wound dangerous, on which she entreated him to leave her to her fate, and to devote himself to those for whose recovery there was rational ground of hope. She was carried to Dannenberg, where, under the most painful agonies, but with the most perfect composure of mind, she expired on the second day.—See Richter, i. p. 477.

[1] The inhabitants of the Old Mark, or westernmost march of Brandenburg. The name indicates the ancient limits of the German empire, and the boundaries of the Sclavonic and German races.

plea of personal history or qualities, might not claim peculiar distinction. And so free were they from all prejudices of class, so jealous in a high self-respect, that no person was admitted into their number who refused to serve as a common Jäger. Their fame has remained. Among the printed records of the war, a separate volume eternizes the exploits of a small body of not more than 3400 warriors.'[1]

So much for one division of Wallmoden's 'CA-NAILLE;' but we are not to imagine that in this eulogy lies the grand secret of Marshal Davoust's inactivity. Far from it. Varnhagen von Ense (*Denkwürdigkeiten*, iii. 401) tells us, that there were too many men fit to be officers in this corps; and that, with a less proportion of princes, philosophers, and bards, it would have done more notable service. The fact is, that when the war first burst out in Silesia, Major von Lützow undertook the formation of this corps, with the view of acting in the rear of the retreating French, as a partisan force, and rousing the whole population of Germany, as he scoured along victorious; but more regular and local arrangements having been afterwards effected, Lützow's corps, which should have been the nucleus of a great division of the Allies, and a seminary, as it were, of young

---

[1] Richter, vol. i. p. 465. The title of the work referred to is *Geschichte des Lützowschen Frei-corps* (Berlin, 1826).

officers, lost its significancy in the great tactics of the war—became a little finger instead of a right arm; and, despite of the inspiring presence of Körner and the son of Andrew Hofer, might, by such a scientific mower-down of serried thousands as Napoleon, not improperly be termed a CANAILLE!

The thing which frightened Davoust, if we may hazard a guess on the matter, was the Cossacks. Tettenborn was a man with moustachios more fierce than Blücher's, and studded magnificently with all manner of Austrian and Russian stars; a man also who, as Von Ense tell us, had been honoured (like Madame de Staël) with the special hate of Napoleon, for daring to appear in a polite French drawing-room with these same terrible moustachios.—'I do not think,' says the Emperor, 'that these moustachios square well with this court-dress' (which the Emperor had specially ordered). 'I do not think,' replied Tettenborn coolly, 'that this dress squares well with these moustachios!'—Such a man, nimbly-strong, and adventurously valiant, had, in the spring of the year, drifted from Petersburg to Wilna, from Wilna to Berlin, from Berlin to Hamburg, like a succession of thunder-plumps; and before his presence and his fleet swarms of weather-beaten Cossacks, mounted on 'tiny goat-like steeds,' men seemed to retreat as women do from rain to save their dresses. Here he

A Niche for Körner. 69

was again, in the latter end of August, with the gallant Lützowers and our German legion, and the other motley items of the *canaille*, now standing on the east side of the Stecknitz with an imperturbable front, which made Davoust imagine that his hundreds were thousands; and now wheeling, God knows whither, to the right hand and to the left, intercepting letters,[1] stopping supplies, rifling it through woods and thickets, gifted apparently with ubiquity. This man, we imagine, robbed Davoust of his enterprise and Körner of his laurels. It is a sad story. Here was a Tyrtæus, as noble a one as ancient or modern story can boast, inspired with the purest poetry, striking with the most patriotic sword—and there was literally nothing for him to do! Davoust, checked at the first move, ensconced himself doggedly on the banks of the Ratzeburger-See, unreachable; and, when at length driven out of that position, he shut himself up in Hamburg. Meanwhile Körner was sent out to do what small things were to be done in the way of petty annoyance. He came upon a few waggons one morning, laden

---

[1] Here, perhaps, more immediately the cause of Davoust's inactivity lay. Napoleon says that he was a good marshal, but not of the best. Perhaps he could only act well at Napoleon's arm. Left to himself he became undecided, cautious, inactive.

with munition and provisions for the enemy; the waggon-men were forced to give up the spoil, but not without a price: on their first dispersion, some of them ran into a wood adjoining, and from behind the brushwood laid the impetuous-rushing young horseman low, with a rifle. The base shot pierced to the spine; and a few hours beheld the noblest warrior of the Liberation War breathless; lost for ever to German patriotism and to European literature, in a manner *le plus bêtement du monde*, as Napoleon elegantly said of his own twin-favourite Marshals, Duroc and Bessières, who fell awkwardly in the early part of the campaign. Such is the wicked chance of war!—of modern war, at least, since the introduction of balls and gunpowder, where the event of the contest (so far as the individual is concerned) may have as little to do with valour as honour has with the issue of a duel in high life; and where it may be the cruel lot of a whole line of Agamemnons to stand stupidly and be shot by some poltroon of a Thersites from behind a bush. Körner's life was brief and glorious. That he fell by such a base death is a sad damper to the romance of modern soldiership. It is truly one of the most melancholy histories that military biography records.

We add an interesting trait of patriotism, from the

combat of the Göhrde (16th September), where the Lützowers distinguished themselves greatly:—'Among those who fell at Göhrde, a few days after the death of Körner, the Oberjäger von Berenhorst deserves particular mention. As he was charging the enemy's squares, he received a shot in his side: he checked his speed for a moment; but instantly collecting himself, he wrapt himself in his mantle, and, with the cry, " KÖRNER, DIR NACH!" (Körner, after thee), cheered on his comrades to the charge; when he was struck by another shot in the breast, and instantly fell.' Thus Körner had not fallen in vain: his soul inspired the victorious hussar-charge of the Göhrde, which checkmated Davoust at Hamburg, and opened the whole of Napoleon's left to the irresistible onset of Marshal FORWARDS.

The three songs which we have selected from Körner are at once among the most popular and the most characteristic that could be selected from his works. The first (No. IV.) describes Lützow's celebrated corps, which must be conceived in its original character, as a partisan force, drifting, Cossack-like, in the rear of the French army, in their retreat from Moscow, and rousing the heart of Germany to the great combat that was to follow. The other words, which we have given to the same air, are not Körner's. We do not know the author; but their historical, if

A Niche for Körner.

not their poetical value, seemed to entitle them to preservation.

The second (No. V.) presents one of the most sublime unions of the devotional and the war-element in poetry that any literature can boast. The third (No. VI.) is universally known; it was composed by the poet only a few hours before his death. Mrs. Hemans has made it, in name at least, familiar to every reader of English poetry—

> 'A song for the death of the brave!
> A song of pride!
> The youth went down to a hero's grave,
> With the SWORD his BRIDE!

WAS GLÄNZT DORT VOM WALDE?

LÜTZOW'S WILD CHASE.

(*Composed at Leipzig, on the Schneckenberg, 24th April* 1813.)

Melody IV.

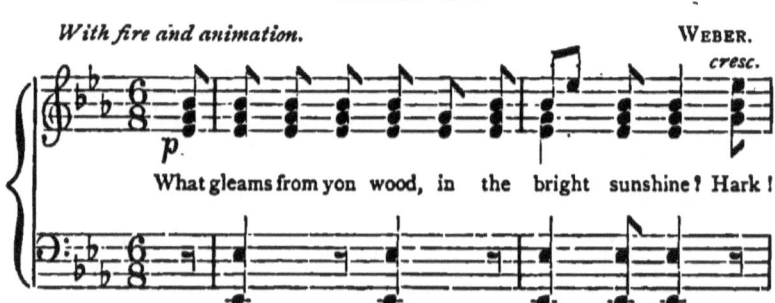

A Niche for Körner.

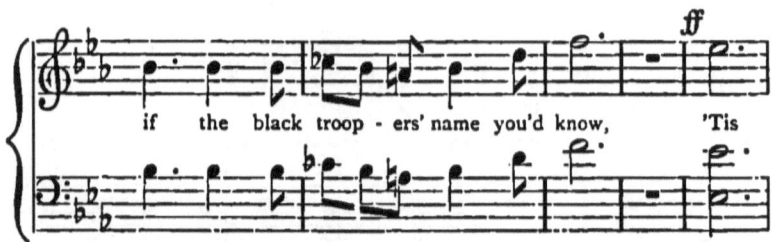

What gleams from yon wood, in the bright sunshine?
  Hark! nearer and nearer 'tis sounding;
It hurries along, black line upon line,
And the shrill-voiced horns in the wild chase join,
  The soul with dark horror confounding:
And if the black troopers' name you'd know,
'Tis Lützow's wild Jäger—a-hunting they go!

From hill to hill, through the dark wood they hie,
  And warrior to warrior is calling;
Behind the thick bushes in ambush they lie,
The rifle is heard, and the loud war-cry,
  In rows the Frank minions are falling:
And if the black troopers' name you'd know,
'Tis Lützow's wild Jäger—a-hunting they go!

A Niche for Körner.

Where the bright grapes glow, and the Rhine rolls wide,
    He weened they would follow him never ;
But the pursuit came like the storm in its pride,
With sinewy arms they parted the tide,
    And reached the far shore of the river :
And if the dark swimmers' name you'd know,
'Tis Lützow's wild Jäger—a-hunting they go!

How roars in the valley the angry fight ;
    Hark! how the keen swords are clashing!
High-hearted Ritter are fighting the fight,
The spark of Freedom awakens bright,
    And in crimson flames it is flashing :
And if the dark Ritters' name you'd know,
'Tis Lützow's wild Jäger—a-hunting they go!

Who gurgle in death, 'mid the groans of the foe,
    No more the bright sunlight seeing?
The writhings of death on their face they show,
But no terror the hearts of the freemen know,
    For the Frantzmen are routed and fleeing :
And if the dark heroes' name you'd know,
'Tis Lützow's wild Jäger—a-hunting they go!

The chase of the German, the chase of the free,
    In hounding the tyrant we strained it!
Ye friends, that love us, look up with glee!
The night is scattered, the dawn we see,
    Though we with our life's-blood have gained it!
And from sire to son the tale shall go :
'Twas Lützow's wild Jäger that routed the foe!

SONG IN CELEBRATION OF THE BATTLE OF LEIPZIG, 18TH OCT. 1813.

(*To the same Air.*)

WHAT fires from the night-clad far heights flare,
   Like flames from the altar ascending?
A burden of prophecy hangs on the air,
As a heralding angel were treading there,
   And voices of triumph are blending:
On night's dark wings rides Victory—
Leipzig, sing ye! sing ye the fight of the free!

Our hoary sires of the ancient day,
   When Varus was routed by Hermann,
The Kaisers that taught haughty Rome to obey,
That hunted the Huns and the Turks away,
   And made Europe free by the German:
They echo the strain with solemn glee,
Leipzig's thunder pealeth—the nations are free!

Brave hearts, that believed in bright freedom's day,
   When Deutschland in slavery languished,
Who at Lützen, at Bautzen, stood stiffly at bay,
Till Dennewitz covered the Frank with dismay,
   Who at Katzbach the elements vanquished;
The hope of your hearts your eyes now see,
Leipzig, sing ye!—Leipzig and Germany free!

And they in the dubious morn who fell
   In fight for the land of their fathers,

A Niche for Körner. 77

The praise of the valiant our hymns shall tell,
And when our tongues name whom we loved so well,
   The fire in our bosom gathers;
While they from heaven's high canopy,
Sing triumphant—Germany, Europe, is free!

Ye sons of strong sires, who for Germany stood,
   When the axe was uplifted to smite her,
Where God marks the spot to the brave and the good,
This night be the oath of the freeman renewed,
   While mounts the flame higher and brighter!
No more shall the tyrant rule Germany!
Leipzig's name shall pledge her for ever—THE FREE.

Then bright may the flame from the dark heights shine!
   The fire in our hearts brighter flameth!
Let German with German in brotherhood join,
Till the Frank shall remeasure his step from the Rhine,
   And his pride the fell Corsican tameth!
And aye as ye march with triumphal glee,
Leipzig, sing ye!—Germany, Fatherland, FREE!

A Niche for Körner.

VATER ICH RUFE DICH!
KÖRNER'S BATTLE PRAYER.
MELODY V.

A Niche for Körner.

Father, I call on thee!
Clouds from the thunder-voiced cannon enveil me,
Lightnings are flashing, death's thick darts assail me;
   Ruler of battles, I call on thee!
      Father, O lead thou me!

      Father, O lead thou me!
Lead me to victory, or to death lead me;
With joy I accept what thou hast decreed me.
   God, as thou wilt, so lead thou me!
      God, I acknowledge thee!

      God, I acknowledge thee!
Where, in still autumn, the sear leaf is falling,
Where peals the battle its thunder appalling;
   Fount of all grace, I acknowledge thee!
      Father, O, bless thou me!

      Father, O bless thou me!
Into thy hand my soul I resign, Lord;
Deal, as thou wilt, with the life that is thine, Lord.
   Living or dying, O bless thou me!
      Father, I praise thy name!

A Niche for Körner.

Father, I praise thy name!
Not for earth's wealth or dominion contend we;
The holiest rights of the freeman defend we.
    Victor or vanquished, praise I thee!
        God, in thy name I trust!

        God, in thy name I trust!
When in loud thunder my death-note is knelling,
When from my veins the red blood is welling,
    God, in thy holy name I trust!
        Father, I call on thee!

DU SCHWERDT AN MEINER LINKEN.
THE SWORD SONG.
Melody VI.

Thou sword so cheer-ly shin-ing, What
are thy gleams di-vin-ing? Look'st like a friend on me;

A Niche for Körner.

Triumphs my soul in thee. Hur-rah! hurrah! hur-rah

Thou sword so cheerly shining,
What are thy gleams divining?
Look'st like a friend on me,
Triumphs my soul in thee.
    Hurrah! hurrah! hurrah!

'I love my brave knight dearly,
Therefore I shine so cheerly.
Borne by a gallant knight,
Triumphs the sword so bright.'
    Hurrah! etc.

Yes, trusty sword, I love thee;
A true knight thou shalt prove me.
Thee, my beloved, my bride,
I'll lead thee forth in pride.
    Hurrah! etc.

---

[1] To relish the measure of this poem, the reader must attend to the music. The first two lines are accented on every second syllable; the metrical series being preceded by a start-syllable. The second two lines are more wild and rapid; and, setting out with a dash from the accent, proceed by threes. The *hurrah* is accompanied with the clashing of swords. So *real* songs are sung; not *shams*, such as we dress up for our drawing-rooms.

A Niche for Körner.

' My iron-life, clear raying,
I gave it to thy swaying.
Oh, come, and fetch thy bride !
Lead, lead me forth in pride !'
    Hurrah ! etc.

The festal trump is blaring,
The bridal dance preparing.
When cannon shakes the glen,
I 'll come and fetch thee then.
    Hurrah ! etc.

' Oh, blest embrace that frees me !
My hope impatient sees thee.
Come, bridegroom, fetch thou me ;
Waits the bright wreath for thee ?'
    Hurrah ! etc.

Why in thy sheath art ringing,
Thou iron-soul, fire-flinging ?
So wild with battle's glee,
Why ray'st thou eagerly ?
    Hurrah ! etc.

' I in my sheath am ringing ;
I from my sheath am springing ;
Wild, wild with battle's glee,
Ray I so eagerly.'
    Hurrah ! etc.

Remain, remain within, love ;
Why court the dust and din, love ?

A Niche for Körner.

Wait in thy chamber small,
Wait till thy true knight call.
    Hurrah! etc.

'Then, speed thee, true knight, speed thee!
To love's fair garden lead me;
Show me the roses red,
Death's crimson-blooming bed.'
    Hurrah! etc.

Then, from thy sheath come free thee!
Come, feed mine eye to see thee!
Come, come, my sword, my bride,
I lead thee forth in pride!
    Hurrah! etc.

'How glorious is the free air!
How whirls the dance with glee there!
Glorious, in sun arrayed,
Gleams, bridal-bright, the blade.'
    Hurrah! etc.

Then up, true Ritter German!
Ye gallant sons of Hermann!
Beats the knight's heart so warm,
With 's true love in his arm;
    Hurrah! etc.

With stolen looks divining,
Thou, on my left, wert shining.

Now on my right, my bride,
God leads thee forth in pride.
    Hurrah ! etc.

Then press a kiss of fire on
The bridal mouth of iron.
Woe now or weal betide,
Cursed whoso leaves his bride !
    Hurrah ! etc.

Then break thou forth in singing,
Thou iron-bride, fire-flinging !
Walk forth in joy and pride !
Hurrah ! thou iron-bride !
    Hurrah ! hurrah ! hurrah !

III.

THE RHINE BOUNDARY.

'And it came to pass after these things, that Naboth the Jezreelite had a vineyard, which was in Jezreel, hard by the palace of Ahab king of Samaria. And Ahab spake unto Naboth, saying, Give me thy vineyard, that I may have it for a garden of herbs, because it is near unto my house: and I will give thee for it a better vineyard than it; or, if it seem good to thee, I will give thee the worth of it in money. And Naboth said to Ahab, The Lord forbid it me, that I should give the inheritance of my fathers unto thee.'—1 KINGS XXI. 1-3.

IT has always appeared to me that of all virtues the most difficult for our frail human nature to practise is JUSTICE. In regard specially to the present war betwixt Germany and France, I have observed in some quarters the strongest perversion of the judicial faculty. People judge without knowing the circumstances of the case; from pure accidental sympathy with this side of the Rhine, or with that; without even knowing the parties or the case sometimes. For who are the parties? Not France and Prussia certainly, but France and Germany; and this single fact ought at once to dispose of a whole host of prejudices which certain people cherish against the hosts which the statesmanship of Bismarck and the strategy of von Moltke have conducted hitherto with such brilliant success against the French. Prussia, these persons say, is now, and has always been, an aggressive power; it is a violent and an unscrupulous power; a power which has grown great by robbery: we can have no sympathy with robbers. How far this charge is true I am not careful at present to inquire. What quarrels might have been dragging on their slow length between the Prussian monarchs and the red-tapists of the German Empire under Austrian influence, which Frederick the Great in the Seven Years' War took sudden occasion to cut short by the sword; what frettings and grumblings of German people under Danish rule may have led to the curtailment of that already too small Cimbric monarchy on the Baltic, and to the prostration of Austrian influence in Deutschland by the needle-guns of Sadowa; what right or wrong there lay in these and other quarrels, by which the little sandy waste of Brandenburg, originally a mere outlying province of a vast Teutonic empire, has grown up by a few rapid strides into a position of European importance for the present, and significant apprehension for the future—with these questions, in passing my judgment on the right and wrong of the present war, and on the

The Rhine Boundary. 87

conditions of peace that may possibly result from it, I have nothing to do; so long as I am certain, and can show by a long historical deduction, that the present invasion of Germany by the legions of Gaul, which has been so gallantly repelled, is only the last of a long series of invasions which vainglorious, ambitious, and unscrupulous France has made, not against Prussia, but against the unity of the German people and the integrity of the German Empire. That Empire indeed, by the strong hand of the great Napoleon, was, in the first years of the present century, struck to the ground; and deservedly so: it had long ceased to perform the duties of fatherly protection to the German people, having made itself altogether incapable of performing this function, partly by family and dynastic preferences adverse to general German interests, partly by the want of energy and enterprise and intelligent progress in the traditional spirit of its government; but the reins which fell from the feeble hands of the house of Lorraine have been seized by the intelligent vigour of the young Prussian monarchy; and it was against Prussia now, as the head of Germany, that France made war, just as in the time of Charles V. it invaded Austria, not because it hated Austria, but because it wished to weaken Germany. Of this assertion it is the business of the present chapter to bring detailed proof, in order specially that the reader may feel, when he is singing the famous national songs about the Rhine boundary, that he is not indulging merely in a whiff of patriotic sentiment, but that he is giving voice to the grave verdict of Providence in a matter of indisputable right and uncontroverted fact. Our Jacobite songs, inimitable in their way, are inferior in this, that they were made in a bad cause, and against all reasonable hope of success; they were the most brilliant specimens that the world has yet seen of poetry without policy and sentiment without sense; but the stirring German strains which claim the Rhine as a German river, and not as a French boundary-line, however inferior in dramatic picturesqueness and in fine popular pathos, have unquestionably this one great advantage, that they are the expression not only of patriotic sentiment, but of historical fact, natural right, and wise policy.

I suppose no person requires to be told that the affair of the Spanish crown was only the occasion, not the cause, of the recent aggressive act of France on Germany. The great French nation felt itself insulted, forsooth, because the King of Prussia would not allow himself to be dictated to in reference to the possibilities of the possession of the Spanish throne by a member of the Hohenzollern family in all time coming! A more flagrant act of insolence by one great power towards another can hardly be conceived. The King of Prussia, as any monarch who had the slightest regard for his dignity must have done, refused to submit to such demands; forthwith the indignation of the great nation flamed up, like the eager sense of honour in the heart of a foolish young duellist, and war was declared. But no man imagines that the hot Frenchman in all this was a mere gasconader; he did not take offence so seriously at such a trifle; but his pride was touched that a German should presume to look a Frank in the face, and he was glad that a new occasion had suddenly flashed into existence for realizing his old ambitious dream of the Rhine boundary. This was unquestionably the feeling of the French people, or at least of that part of the French people which in public and political matters has always assumed the right of thinking and acting for the whole nation. As to the Emperor, we may well suppose that he had sense enough to know that the conqueror of Sadowa was not a man to be meddled with rashly in military matters; but that desire for popularity, and the itch for foreign occupation, and the necessity of success, which together form the Nemesis of every usurper, forced him into the current of military insolence, and he was driven by it, with uncertain, and we may well believe half-unwilling, steps into his ruin. As for Prussia, some have blamed her monarch for being forward to 'speak the decisive word' and to fling down the gauntlet. I blame her not. In the political world the man who submits to be kicked will very soon be flogged, and the people which has once patiently been flogged, only waits another turn of the wheel to be flayed. Of this Germany had large experience in her transactions with the French monarchs of the sixteenth and seventeenth centuries; and in public as in private life, the only way to command respect from a highwayman is to knock him down. The German people had not now for the first time to learn the ambitious rapacity of the French. They were perfectly aware that that people was eagerly waiting its opportunity for an act of aggression; that war sooner or later was inevitable with a neighbour so disposed; and that it was better to finish it at once with a grand blow, than to keep fretting on from year to year, and maintaining a constant organization of defence little less expensive than the cost of an immediate war. Like wise men, Bismarck and Moltke were ready; they did not sleep with open doors and windows when a burglar was whetting his tools before their eyes; and, with no less wisdom than courage determined that, though they would not attack their hereditary enemy till provoked, they

The Rhine Boundary. 91

would, when provoked, show no backwardness to commence the fray. All this was exactly what should have been, provided their motive to action was consistent with fact; that is to say, provided the French had really always practised an aggressive policy towards Germany, and had in nowise relinquished it now. That such an aggressive policy has always inspired France we shall now proceed to prove.

The declaration of war, we have already said, was made for the purpose of humbling Prussia, and giving the Rhine boundary to France. Let us look first into the historical roots of this extraordinary claim. The ancient Roman and Greek writers, in a general sort of way, no doubt, say that the river Rhine separates Gaul from Germany,[1] but these very writers tell us with sufficient distinctness that this general line of demarcation did not, even in the days of the great Roman dictator, express the actual state of the fact any more than it does at the present day. No fact in history is more certain than that in the days of the first Roman emperors, and even of Julius Cæsar himself, a population of essentially German extraction occupied

---

[1] 'Belgæ proximi sunt Germanis, qui trans Rhenam incolunt.' —Cæsar, *B. G.* i. 1.

'Germania omnis a Gallis, Rhætisque et Pannoniis Rheno et Danubio fluminibus separatur.'—Tac. *de Mor. Germ.* i. 1.

most parts of the left bank of the Rhine. The Tribocci who possessed Alsace were certainly Germans; and the Treviri, who occupied the modern Treves, no less; it is impossible, indeed, to say how much German population was mixed up with that division of Gaul which Cæsar designates 'Belgæ.'[1] In those days, when barbarian tribes like April showers were drifting from the east one upon the back of the other, into the half-peopled regions of the west, how can any thinking man imagine that a river, or even a firth of the sea, would form a marked boundary which a Celtic or Teutonic race of men would never think of passing? Those who live on the indented coast of our West Highlands know that long arms of the sea, so far from barring local communication, rather facilitate it; for few things are easier to make than a raft or a boat; and those who live in these counties move much more fre-

---

[1] 'Plerosque Belgas esse ortos ab Germanis, Rhenumque antiquitus transductos propter loci fertilitatem ibi consedisse.' —Cæsar, *B. G.* ii. 4.

'Treviri et Nervii circa affectationem Germanicæ originis ultro ambitiosi sunt; Ipsam Rheni ripam haud dubie Germanorum populi colunt, Vangiones, Triboci, Nemetes.'—Tac. *de Mor. Germ.* 28.

Μετὰ δὲ 'Ελουηττίους Σηκοανοὶ καὶ Μεδιοματρικοὶ κατοικοῦσι τὸν 'Ρῆνον, ἐν οἷς ἵδρυται Γερμανικὸν ἔθνος περαιωθὲν ἐκ τῆς οἰκείας Τρίβοκχοι.—Strabo, iv. 193, c.

quently and much more readily on the water than on the land. The land on both sides of a river—like Tweeddale or Strathtay—is generally part of a natural district, which the river connects, not disjoins. A race of people who had settled on the east side of a fertile river plain would be altogether blind if they did not see that to ferry themselves over to the west section of the same territory is the plainest sequence of a natural right to be where they are. It is not rivers that separate diverse races of men, but mountains, as the Alps, the Pyrenees, the Carpathians, and the Grampians sufficiently indicate; and it is, independently of all historical testimony, as improbable that the Rhine should have separated the Gauls from the Germans in the days of the Cæsars, as that the river Forth should mark the boundary between the Celtic and the Lowland population of Scotland at the present day. Not the Forth, or even the Tay, but the 'Mons Grampius,' at whose foot Galgacus fought, marks the boundary which nature and history have fixed between the Celtic and Teutonic races in Scotland; so in Alsatia not the Rhine, but the Vosges, is at once the natural and the historical boundary of France; or, if this is not the natural boundary, then certainly before they can find another equally natural, the French must go beyond the Rhine and occupy all the plain that lies to the east of that noble river, and the highlands of Swabia and the Schwarzwald. But obvious as all this is, that lust of conquest which is the besetting sin of all strong governments, led the French, even before the first scenes of what is commonly called modern history, to lay claim to the Rhine as the natural boundary of their country, and to make its acquisition the aim of a perfidious and rapacious policy continued during the space of four centuries. No sooner, in fact, did Charles VII., by the truce of Tours in 1444, find himself relieved from the constant fret of the English wars in the west of his dominions, than he set himself to put the wedge into the first gap that he could find in the huge broadside of the German Empire, as a means for the appropriation of Alsace and Lorraine, and the other German territories that lay beyond the natural boundary of France, and between that boundary and the Rhine. An opportunity for this was soon presented by the quarrels which were at that time running their fretful course between Frederick III. the Austrian Emperor, and the stout mountaineers of the Swiss rural cantons. Frederick, too weak to combat these stalwart peasants with the means at his own disposal, sent his secretary Æneas Sylvius with an urgent request to Charles to send him some of his recently disbanded soldiers, to help him to put down the Swiss. With this request the French monarch complied with an eagerness beyond the expectation and the wish of the Emperor. It was the old story of the horse asking the man to help it, with which the man complied by mounting on the animal's back and refusing to be unseated. Two armies were accordingly sent to the Rhine, one commanded by the King, the other by the Dauphin—with the success or failure of which, on the present occasion, we have nothing to do; but what concerns us to note is the language in which this proceeding is mentioned by Martin, a recent and well accredited historian of France:—'On disait hautement autour de Charles VII. qu'il fallait *profiter des circonstances, pour revendiquer les anciens droits de la couronne de France sur tous les pays situés en deçà du Rhin.* Ainsi la France reprenait déjà *son éternelle tendance vers les limites de la Gaule.*'[1] This single passage is the key to the whole history of France through Louis XIV. up to the great Napoleon, and the present astonishing explosion of national ignorance, arrogance, and conceit. French ambition wishes to occupy the Rhine; therefore it believes the lie that this river is its natural boundary; and its whole

---

[1] *Histoire de la France*, par Henri Martin (Paris, 1855), tom. vi. p. 414. The exact words of Æneas Sylvius, Epist. 87, are quoted by the modern historian.

policy, which shall make its Richelieus, and Louises, and Napoleons famous, is 'to profit by circumstances,' for the purpose of getting hold of what does not belong to it. It is the old Hebrew Ahab with a new name, determined to attach Naboth's vineyard, by fair means if possible, and if not, by foul. This is an overture to a military-diplomatic opera of four centuries, so significant and so prophetic, that the whole of the drama which follows, as in the plays of Euripides, can be spelt out from the prologue. You see the foot of Hercules here fully displayed, and you may gather surely from this what a neck the oaf has, and what a gorge. Let us see how the play goes on. The great wars of the sixteenth and the first half of the seventeenth century were religious in their origin, and political only by the necessary admixture of politics with every movement that stirs great masses of men, and asserts large social claims. The Protestant Reformation caused more innocent blood to be shed in Europe than the ambition of many kings. So it must ever be. The devil is a strong man, and will not yield without a struggle. '*I come not to send peace, but a sword.*' And so it was that the flaming words of mighty truth, flung into the heart of Germany by the volcanic indignation of honest Martin Luther, gained a victory for the truth indeed over the most vigorous and progressive part of

The Rhine Boundary. 97

Europe; but did so only at the expense of a recurrent civil war, which not only divided the German Empire against itself, but exposed it a defenceless prey to the intrigues, the fraud, and the rapacity of its neighbours. The first act of the great drama of dismemberment took place in the year 1552, when the three bishoprics of Metz, Toul, and Verdun, which formed part of the German Empire, were appropriated by France. The occasion of this robbery was the imperial obstinacy of Charles V., which led him to force a palliated Popery down the throats of the Germans, and thus raise up an enemy among those of his own household, who was more than a match for his master in all those arts of dissimulation, by the exercise of which weakness has so often contrived to gain a victory over strength. Maurice of Saxony was a man who knew how to use that wisdom of the ancient Greeks, which taught them 'when the lion's hide would not do, to put on the fox's skin;' but, though he was superior to Charles by a mastery in such wiles, he was not strong enough to strike a decisive blow alone. He had therefore recourse to France; and brought in Henry II. to checkmate the Emperor and to 'profit by circumstances' for the attainment of the coveted Rhine boundary. Nothing could possibly have sounded more pious and virtuous, patriotic and philanthropic, than the manifesto with which Henry entered on this war. To have made an honest bargain, that as the reward of his services against the Emperor he should be invested with the sovereignty of the three bishoprics, would not have suited his purpose. Maurice was too good a German to have connived at this; and, besides, he had no power to grant it. He only agreed to the French stipulation, that if it were found necessary to elect a new emperor, such a person should be nominated as would be agreeable to the king of France.[1] The manifesto accordingly sounded the note of war in the most noble and disinterested key. The king of France came on the stage as the protector of the liberties of Germany, and of its captive princes; and the symbol of a cap between two daggers showed visibly to the Teutonic people that not for the subjugation or spoliation of the fatherland, but only for the chastisement of Austro-Spanish insolence, had chivalrous France unsheathed the sword. As for religion, that was wisely not mentioned. That the head of the Church in a Catholic country, who persecuted Protestantism at home, should have undertaken a war for the purpose of protecting Protestantism abroad, was enough to show the essential hollowness and selfishness of the alliance; but those

---

[1] Robertson's *Charles V.*, ch. x. anno 1551.

The Rhine Boundary. 99

who made war had at least the grace not to profess in words a zeal for that religion whose interests they were practically disregarding. The whole transaction was political; and the transparent motive of it was not the defence of Protestant liberties in Germany, but the weakening of the German Empire by dissension, and the advance to the coveted Rhine boundary by a well-calculated combination of diplomatic fraud and military violence. The movement was successful. Metz was taken by what a grave historian has not scrupled to designate as a '*fraudulent* stratagem,'[1] and from that hour to the present, when the avenging Nemesis has come down upon them in the shape of von Moltke, they have never loosed their grip from this dishonourable capture.

The foreign policy of France in the brilliant epochs which followed during the next three centuries, was merely a repetition on a grander scale of the system of aggression just characterized. It was like the recurrent eruptions of a volcano, which, after slackening a certain time, is sure to break out again, and which, when it does break out, always sends the devastating lava-stream in the same favourite direc-

---

[1] Robertson, as above, anno 1552. The details will be found in *Elsass und Lothringen; nachweis wie diese Provinzen dem Deutschen Reiche verloren gingen,* von Professor Adolf Schmidt. Dritte Auflage (Leipzig, 1870). A valuable sketch.

tion. The first, and upon the whole the most reputable, of those Gallic eruptions, took place in the middle of the seventeenth century, under the administration of Cardinal Richelieu—a great man certainly, if, as in the case of the great Napoleon, mere intellectual and volitional force can be justly looked upon as constituting human greatness; but, if moral considerations also must come into the reckoning, one of the smallest. The most terrible and fearfully unhuman of all creatures is a monster, half-tiger, half-fox, under the cassock of a Christian priest; and, bating his high intellect and lofty will, this is just the combination which the character of Richelieu seems to present to the student of political ethics. For what is called conscience in normally constituted men, it is vain to look among persons of this type, in whom the passion for political power has absorbed every feeling that teaches a man to weep with those who weep, and rejoice with those who rejoice. Of himself, Napoleon said truly, 'I love not wine, I love not women, I love not dice; I am altogether a political animal;'[1] and in the same spirit, when Richelieu was on his deathbed, and asked by the attendant priest to forgive his enemies, he answered firmly, 'Richelieu has no enemies but

---

[1] *Memoirs of Lord Holland.*

those of the state;[1] which, being interpreted into common language, merely meant that whatever crimes he might have committed, which in private men would have been condemned as revenge and murder, were in his case to be praised as patriotism, for they were all committed for the preservation of his power—a power in his estimate identical with the salvation, or at least the aggrandizement, of his country. The moral attitude of Richelieu towards Protestant Germany was the same as that of Henry III.; it presented the monstrous spectacle of a Christian priest of the highest dignity spending magazines of money and shedding oceans of blood for the protection of that faith abroad which he persecuted, and as a consistent Romanist was bound to persecute, at home. Such indeed was the utter hollowness, systematic mendacity, and organized duplicity of the policy of France in those days, that the great Richelieu is found coolly subsidizing the Protestant king of Sweden and the Catholic duke of Bavaria, fighting on opposite sides, in the same year.[2] But however abhorrent to every instinct of a healthy humanity the spirit of such a policy might be, and however impure the motives which induced Richelieu to follow out the hereditary aggressive policy of his country in the direction of

---

[1] Crowe, *History of France*, vol. iii. p. 540.
[2] *Ibid.* vol. iii. p. 505.

Germany during the woful period of the Thirty Years' War, it must at the same time be honestly admitted, that if the Cardinal's wars and intrigues ended, in making Lorraine and Alsace virtually, though not yet in all respects legally and rightfully, a part of the French Empire, the Germans, on the other hand, certainly have no reason to complain that they did not get on that occasion a *quid pro quo* sufficient to absolve the Cardinal from the charge of open rapacity and unblushing perfidy which attaches to the name of Louis XIV. For in the progress of that long-drawn chain of civil miseries it became painfully apparent, that without calling in foreign aid, Protestant Germany was not strong enough to contend against the Catholic imperialism of the south; and, as the war went on, it seemed morally certain that the rights of conscience would speedily be stamped out in Saxony and Brandenburg, just as they had been in Bohemia. To avert this terrible calamity, the Swedes and the French were called in; and if the one paid themselves at the peace of Westphalia by settling in Pomerania, and the other by occupying Alsace, it seemed the necessary price of their assistance. No nation can afford to spend blood and treasure for another out of pure generosity. So far, therefore, the German people seem to stand under a plain obligation to Richelieu; and for the loss of Alsace at that period they have to blame the blindness of their own Emperor as much as the rapacity of the French minister. But the case alters altogether when we pass on to the next famous epoch of Gallic aggrandizement, the age of Louis XIV. Here we have a scene presented to our view more like the wild outburst of some Asiatic scheme of conquest than the reign of law which we are accustomed to praise in civilized European monarchies. The idea of combined brute force and vulpine cunning which had incarnated itself in the Christian priest Richelieu, now found its more natural and more magnificent avatar in the person of an absolute secular monarch, with whom from the beginning law meant nothing but will, and will nothing but vainglory and rapacity. Historians have brought to light the extremely significant little educational fact, that when this magnificent Louis was being taught writing, the copy placed before him under the letter R was—'*Les Rois font tout ce qu'ils veulent;*'[1] and from the germ of such early precept to such a pupil what but the most gigantic and all-grasping selfishness could be the growth? A mighty monarch was launched upon the stage of Christian Europe, who coolly considered that he had a right to whatever he

---

[1] Crowe, iii. p. 647.

wished to take, and who in his public transactions with Christian peoples never scrupled at any promise that it was convenient for him to make to-day and profitable to break to-morrow. The extraordinary pretensions which, after the death of the smooth and subtle Mazarin, grew up in the breast of this spoiled prince, like splendid scarlet fungi out of rank rottenness, are to our sober and moral view of things with difficulty conceivable. In regard to Germany, the favourite dream of the Rhine boundary to the imagination of young Louis presented an object altogether unworthy of his ambition : Richelieu, who was only a minister and a churchman, not a mighty monarch, had already almost secured that; the advocates of Louis boldly claimed for him all that had belonged eight hundred years before to the Franco-German empire of Charlemagne : the French monarchs, who at that period had their seat of power westward of the Rhine, always extended their sway beyond that river ; France had, in fact, a right of sovereignty over all German countries ; and the acquisitions of Alsace and Lorraine were, in this view, not conquests from the empire, but a just restitution to the ancient crown of France![1] These were not the views of mere rhetorical partisans—lawyers, priests, courtiers, diplo-

---

[1] Crowe, iii. p. 658.

matists, or by whatsoever title the servile crew, ready worshippers of the rising sun, might happen to be named; they were the actual principles on which this brilliant robber acted, and of which his whole life (called by historians 'glorious') is an exposition. Fortunately, however, for Germany, Flanders presented a more open field for nefarious appropriation. Here too he found a more specious excuse for his robbery. His Spanish wife's dowry had not been fully paid, and he could seize Spanish Flanders as a compensation for that deficit; or he would bribe lawyers to prove that the lady was the rightful heir of that part of the Spanish dominions; and when monarchical knaveries require to be committed, lawyers and priests have always been at hand to give a respectable authority and a sacred sanction to fraud. So the thunder of the Zeus Olympius of Versailles burst principally on Flanders, and thereafter on Holland; brilliantly enough at first, no doubt, but with comparatively small profit in the end; for in Europe, as Heeren justly remarks,[1] there was no room for such an Asiatic swoop of the sword; and, like Napoleon afterwards, the omnipotent Louis, crossed and thwarted by a thousand petty combinations, might have frequent cause to lament that he

---

[1] Staaten-system. *Staatshändel in Europe*, 1661-1700, t. i.

had missed his destiny in not being born a Tamerlane or a Genghis Khan. Holland escaped, and Belgium was only partially scathed; but a final nail required to be driven into the somewhat loose jointwork by which the greater part of Lorraine and Alsace had been incorporated with France; and Louis was just the man to do it. For this purpose, by way of novelty, or because wars were too expensive, he hired lawyers, and created 'chambers of reunion' to prove, by the refurbishing of fusty old papers, and the application of all sorts of unreal fictions, that certain places which were at that time legally part of the German empire had been forfeited to France. This was the same card which had been so dexterously played by the English king Edward I. to prove that Scotland was a rightful fief of the English crown; a claim which met with the only proper answer from Bruce at Bannockburn, but which, when made by Louis XIV. against the German Empire, was allowed to pass, not, of course, because anybody felt that it was right, but because Germany, fallen already into two opposite camps, instead of a king to fight its battles, had only a philosopher to teach its duties. This philosopher was Leibnitz, who in the month of August 1670, at Swalbach, declared himself as follows :—'Germany, like Greece once, and Italy later, is the great apple of contention with the world.

The Rhine Boundary.

It is the ball for those who play at monarchy, and the battle-field for those who contest it. The first duty of patriotism is to rescue the common fatherland from being made either the plaything of diplomacy or the field of the war-struggle. *The princes have but to unite in order to render Germany invincible.*[1] But these wise words could be of no avail so long as the head of the German empire was a monarch whose position and interests led him rather to cultivate Popish friendship in the south, and to fear Turkish aggression in the east, than to defend the Protestant interest in north-western Germany against the ambition of the French monarchs. Louis accordingly, a few years afterwards, seized a favourable moment to appropriate Strasburg; an act of pure robbery, for which scarcely the most cunning lawyers sitting in royal 'chambers of reunion' might be able to forge a vindication. Louis in fact for himself required no vindication; it was only the foolish honest world for whom vindications required to be trumped up. A king is a person who does whatever he pleases; and it pleased this modern Ahab of the Seine on this occasion to take hold of the vineyard of the German Naboth, which looked so like as if it naturally ought to belong to him.

---

[1] Leibnitz, Bedenken de securitate publica; *apud* Crowe's *France*, iii. p. 675.

This was in the year 1681; and two years afterwards, when the Turk, with whom the most Christian monarch warmly sympathized, was closely pressing Vienna, this brilliant robber was looking down across the Rhine, like a vulture, eager to pounce on his expected victim; for, had the Turks prevailed and Poland not sent forth an unexpected champion in the person of John Sobieski, it was his Majesty's royal intention either to have partitioned the Empire or claimed the German crown for the Dauphin! I wonder if Bossuet, and the other court-preachers of that time, ever told Louis that robbery was inconsistent with Christianity. If they did not, they were poor creatures compared with the old Hebrew prophets, who never feared to rebuke a crowned sinner to his face; and the Christianity which they preached as an engine of social reform proved itself vastly inferior to the Judaism which it had supplanted.

It is not necessary for the readers of these sketches to enter into any detail of the German policy of the great Napoleon. That may be presumed to be fresh in the memory of every educated reader; and the Titanic commotions with which it was attended are even now felt coursing the veins and thrilling the nerves of every man who takes an interest in the history of his kind. One sees here only a repetition of the ambitious schemes of Louis, starting from a different basis, inspired by a different idea, and spreading over a much ampler space. It was the fashion, no doubt, for the Liberal party in this country, when they were in opposition and obliged to contradict the Tory ministry in all matters, to assert that there would have been no French invasion of Europe, as a consequence of the great revolution of 1789, had the Whig principle of non-intervention been acted upon by England and the other European powers; but no impartial student of history, looking back on these times calmly from the present hour, can for a moment deceive himself into an illusion of this kind. True, it may be that the convention of Pilnitz, the germ of the Prussian invasion of France in 1792, of which poet Goethe has left a record, was a measure calculated to warn France that they had enemies on the east side of the Rhine against whom it were wise to be on their guard; but no man who considers the general vehemence of the French counsels (if such volcanic explosions could be called counsels) at the time, and specially the policy and the practice revealed in the seizure of Savoy, can entertain any reasonable doubt that the French policy, from 1792 downwards, whether under the first genuine democrats or under Napoleon, the masked champion of absolutism, was essentially a policy of aggression and encroachment. How, we may rather ask, could it be otherwise? The French nation at that time was mad (if indeed they are not always suffering under a chronic madness); and madness, when it is not fatuity, but what the lawyers call furiosity, is always aggressive. Another thing also is sufficiently plain: the country which suffered most from this twenty years' system of aggression was Germany. The changes in the internal government of the French people made not the slightest change in the hereditary ambitious schemes which dictated their foreign policy; and the fatherland suffered equally in the body and in the members, whether from the overboiling of the democratic caldron, stirred by the iron ladle of Napoleon, or from the vainglorious dreams of the magnificent Louis, partially realized by the craft of a a despotic churchman and the sword of an unscrupulous soldier. In the summer of the year 1812, as the grand fruit of this gigantic system of European robbery, Germany lay at the feet of Napoleon, and the dreams of Louis XIV. seemed on the point of being realized. In the autumn of 1813, in virtue of a three days' thunder on the plains of Leipzig, matters were reversed; the whole of this mighty structure of Gallic ambition had fallen to the ground like a castle of cards; Germany, inspired by a new patriotic soul, and united by a new spiritual bond, with one strong

The Rhine Boundary. 111

Titanic upheaval rolled Gallic pretension from its imperial seat; and Europe for a space breathed free. But another terrible struggle remained. It was, however, only the last convulsive shock of a departing earthquake; the demon of unrest in the breast of the despotic Corsican and of the foolish French people brought on a final conflict, in which, as might have been prophesied, the frenzied outburst of an unsanctified ambition could not prevail against the grand combination of Celtic chivalry, Scottish persistency, English pluck, and Prussian fervour presented at Waterloo. The combat was now fought out; the volcano was spent; the sword had done its perfect work; and the province of the tongue and the pen commenced. On the 15th July 1815 the diplomatists met at Paris—a place of meeting ominous of evil to Germany, and very favourable to French intrigue—and, as often happens, these heroes of the bureau did not perform their part in the way that seemed the natural sequence of the military scenes which had preceded. It was by the counsels of Stein mainly, and the swords of Blücher and Gneisenau, that the victories had been gained; but it was not their swords that dictated the peace. The claims of the Germans were the main thing which occupied the deliberations of the Congress; and unquestionably, after what they had suffered from French aggression, and what they had achieved by persistent valour, their claims ought to have found favourable ears at that board. But it was quite the reverse: France was the favoured party at the Congress; and if any man had cause to boast of the conditions of that peace, it was neither Hardenberg the Prussian minister, nor Metternich, nor even Wellington and Castlereagh, but that bland old deceiver and arch-juggler, Talleyrand. The members who composed this Congress were only four—Russia, Prussia, England, and France. Here was a gross injustice to the fatherland in the very constitution of the board; there should have been a representative of Bavaria and the other German powers, who had taken part in the war, and suffered most from the depredations of the French hordes of civilized aggressors. The fate of Germany was to be decided; but the voice of Germany was not taken. A board consisting of two foreign members — England and Russia (with Talleyrand and Louis XVIII. at their back)—was sitting in Paris, for the shortest space possible (for Castlereagh told them to be quick); and these, along with Prussia to represent Prussian interests, and Austria to represent Austrian interests, were to decide upon the fate of Germany, whose songs had been sung, and whose blood had been poured out like rivers, not certainly to achieve a diplomatic victory to Talleyrand and the Bourbon. The issue was, what was only too easy to anticipate: 'Diplomatists,' as Capo d'Istria with singular honesty said, 'are not the best sort of men;' and in fact they often have a sort of work to do, in the adjustment of selfish interests, and the dressing-up of deceitful speciosities, which the best sort of men would scorn to soil their fingers with. The only hope for Germany in a council so composed was, that Prussia and Austria, as they had fought together at Leipzig for the common Teutonic liberty, so they should now take counsel together for the common Teutonic right; for that England and Russia would stand forward with any forwardness for the rights of Germany was more than could be expected from human or diplomatic nature. Russia had not lost any territory by French aggression, and so had nothing to revindicate; England had been threatened, and a little frightened, but was never attacked; safe in their remote strongholds, the one of these powerful States, defended by a cincture of winter frosts, and the other by a girdle of briny waves, could sit at the green table with a lofty unconcern, and dispense what might appear justice to all but the party who had a serious grievance to redress. The justice of the case plainly required, not that the wings of the French eagle should be allowed to spread themselves out in unpruned insolence; but that the people who for more than three hundred years had been systematically plundered should force the rapacious bird to disgorge. Why was this not done? Why were not Alsace and Lorraine, original provinces of the German Empire, wrested from them by the united fraud and force of French governments, and now, by the right of conquest in the hands of the Germans, not allowed to remain in their hands? I have already indicated where the magnet lay that disturbed the polarity of the needle of justice in this case. England and Russia were indifferent to German interests, but they were not indifferent to Louis XVIII. The word 'Legitimacy,' blazoned by Talleyrand, was admirably calculated to divert the representatives of crowned heads from the real points at issue. These points were justice to Germany and safety to Europe; but instead of this, legitimacy meant unmerited courtesy to the Bourbons and unwise deference to French feelings. That Alexander's judgment was warped by this false point of view is possible enough; but over and above this, he had no interest to see a strong Germany, or a strong Prussia, and so opened the proceedings of the Congress by putting in a pleading for France. It was currently believed also at the time, that a certain lady, Madame von Krüdener, very beautiful and very good, had helped the imperial

Muscovite to varnish with a pious gloss his indifference to German interests; and if so, it is not the first occasion on which fair and saintly women, with a magic peculiarly their own, interfering in the stern business of public life, have worked great mischief. Alexander's negative attitude is therefore explained. But what of England? We had spent much money, lost not a little blood, and made a splendid reputation by opposing the aggressions of France; and what did we mean by it? Was it to make a strong France and a weak Germany? or should it not rather have been to make a strong Germany and a weak France? Why, after conquering the robber, did we not treat him as robbers are rightfully treated, by forcing him to return his unjust gains, and making him taste a little of that cup of wrongs which he had so largely administered to others? The words of Castlereagh, as they stand before all Europe in the public acts of the Congress, and the known character of the ministry whom he represented, do, I am afraid, sufficiently explain the feebleness and ineffectiveness of our policy on that occasion. It had got into the head of the gentleman who conducted the English negotiations for peace, that we had been fighting, not for the restoration of the balance of power, destroyed by centuries of French encroachment, but for the restoration of the Bourbons! Therefore not the rights of the German people, as victors at Leipzig, but the dignity of our ally Louis XVIII. as legitimate lord of France, one and indivisible, was the main thing to be considered. Never was a more transparent sophism. What the Tory ministry as a mere English party had been fighting for they best knew, but what the Congress of Paris had to perform, as executors of the legacy of Leipzig and Waterloo, was to redeem the wrongs of Germany in the first place, and, in the second place, to provide real and not illusory guarantees against future aggressions on the part of France. However, Castlereagh, I suspect, was not statesman enough to see this—he was only a Tory; and a great international question of European concern seems to have been treated by him as an affair of dynasty and family feeling. England was thus gained over diplomatically to the interests of that France which she had conquered in the field; and with this cunning bond of Bourbon legitimacy between the two powers who ought to have been impartial, the case of Germany was lost. For the combined action of Austria and Prussia, which alone could have turned the tables, was no longer there; the bloody cement of Leipzig gradually melted away in the diplomatic atmosphere of the Hotel Borghese; the old jealousies showed themselves, or worked wickedly in the background; if it was at one time agreed that Alsace should be restored, it was found out soon that it was difficult to agree whether Baden should get it, or Würtemberg, or mighty Austria; indecision of counsels produced feebleness of action; and so it was at last resolved to trump up a hasty conclusion, and leave Germany altogether out of the question. Prussian patriots, of course, felt sorely aggrieved at this; the practical sagacity of von Stein, the fervid patriotism of Arndt, and the far-sighted wisdom of William von Humboldt, protested loudly against the blunder; but it was too late: Prussia might console herself by being allowed to swallow half of her elder sister, German Saxony, whose crime was weakness, not ambition; while the materials ready for her compensation, the robbed provinces of the German Empire, were allowed to remain in the hands of the victorious vanquished![1]

Europe, now only half pleased with a hasty and partial peace, but heartily sick of a generation of devastating wars, assumed for a long period the attitude of political repose; and Germany retired from her hard-fought fields, with only two guarantees for her future safety against a repetition of her past

---

[1] The materials for forming a sound judgment on the second peace of Paris will be found in *Geschichte des Zweiten Pariser-Friedens*, von Schaumann (Göttingen, 1824), and in Schmidt's work, quoted as above.

dangers from the west—the guarantee of the favoured Bourbon dynasty, and the possibility that the French people, while still in possession of Strasburg, might depart at length from their cherished dream of the Rhine boundary! Alas for poor Germany! these 'moral guarantees,' of which Capo d'Istria loved to talk, proved the one a broken reed, and the other (if any one ever believed in it) a deceitful mirage. The Bourbons went out, and the Orleanists came in, and the Napoleons came back, and Germany was again face to face with an ambitious France, and a people eager mainly to wipe off the disgrace of Waterloo, but not at all grateful for the Anglo-Russian moderation displayed in the second treaty of Paris, and dreaming hot day-dreams, as before, about the Rhine boundary and the right of France to dictate a policy to Europe at the point of the bayonet! How universally the Gallic mind was possessed by these overweening pretensions Germany knew always, and Europe knows now; but to those who are not familiar with the persistency of popular imaginations of national glory, and their indissoluble connection with robbery, the following extract from the school-book of geography officially authorized by France in the government of Louis Philippe may prove instructive:

'*France does not possess its natural boundaries; it does not possess the whole region which properly is part of*

The Rhine Boundary. 119

France. Regions are represented by races and languages. The French region really comprehends Nice, Savoy, Switzerland, Rhenish Bavaria, Rhenish Prussia, and Belgium. The natural boundaries of our country are the Rhine from its source to its mouth."[1] After such precocious˙ indoctrination how could the hopeful scholars of the Polytechnic and other schools of the great nation avoid carrying in their brain-boxes so much gunpowder, ready to explode at the first spark of real or imaginary affront that might be offered to their conceit? And the instructions of the school-books have been only too promptly obeyed. War was declared by France against Prussia for the possession of the Rhine boundary, and for no other purpose; and does any one doubt, if France had been as mighty in the fight as she was forward in the challenge, that she would have hesitated to appropriate the long-coveted territory—and who could have hindered her? Either she would thus gloriously, as she phrases it, have consummated her long career of splendid robberies, or there must have been a European war. Let then Justice be even-handed. If, as the clear-sighted Duke of Wellington plainly saw, the French revolution and the treaty of Paris

---

[1] From Dussieux, *Géographie hist. de la France* (Paris, 1843), in Schmidt, p. 5; and for another testimony to the same effect see *Edinburgh Review*, October 1870, p. 570.

left France in too great strength for the rest of Europe,[1] and if, notwithstanding this admission, he saw himself constrained by circumstances, as he thought, not to curtail that strength then, let it by all means be done now; let retribution wait on the guilty. In such matters there is and can be no prescription; certainly none between parties whose political relation has been so fixed as that between France and Germany for the last three hundred years; and if Europe would have allowed victorious France to appropriate the whole western skirts of Germany, which naturally do not belong to her, let her not express a partial indignation, or exhibit a perverted sympathy, if by the same fortune of war a righteous Providence shall now at length have thrown into the hands of the German people part of that territory which does naturally belong to them. Surely a bloody experience may at length have taught us, that a strong Germany in the centre of Europe is the one keystone that can keep the arch of power steady at once from the slow encroachments of Russia on the east, and the explosive aggressions of France on the west.[2]

---

[1] Despatches, Paris, 11th August 1815.
[2] In revising these words, I find that I have omitted only one point which has a direct practical bearing on the terms of peace, which Bismarck, if he should end as well as he has begun, is wisely entitled to dictate to France. It is said to be

The Rhine Boundary.

This rapid sketch of the French 'tendency towards the Rhine' will, we hope, be sufficient to show the reader from what a deep root of fact the Rhine songs have grown. It is only, indeed, when they spring out of such a strong reality that poetry and music possess that most excellent virtue in national educa-

---

a monstrous thing in these times violently to transfer a people from one ruler to another without their consent. My answer to this is twofold. Supposing, what this objection implies, that the people of Alsace, or a majority of them, is really strongly opposed to reunion with Germany, it is quite plain to me that, as to the effect of such a transference, the people of the country are no adequate judges. What they can judge of is their own momentary inconvenience, arising from the disturbance of certain habits and associations. Human laziness will always be averse to all changes for reasons of this kind; but the mere numerical majority of the Alsatians cannot possibly have any reasonable ground for imagining that the future prosperity of their country would be better insured by joining themselves to the decadent fortunes of France, than to the rising strength of their native Germany. But more than this: the transference of the German provinces of France to their original rulers is really not a provincial and local, but a European question; it is to put a final stop to the ambitious dreams of France with regard to the Rhine boundary, that the restoration to Germany of its natural boundary is demanded. Where such large interests are concerned, the likings or dislikings of the inhabitants of a small district are of no consideration. They must make up their minds in a little matter to do what it is for the good of the whole political body that they should do. It is neither the convenience of Alsace nor even the rights of Germany that are to be considered in the matter, so much as the safety of Europe and the stability of the international structure.

tion, which was attributed to them with such practical sagacity by Plato, Aristotle, and all the wise Greeks. A music divorced from historical fact, and from popular life, however curiously it may entertain the ear, can do nothing to fortify the will, to form the character, or to train the reason; rather, as we have sometimes seen, it may prove the dainty nurse of feebleness and the sweet solace of slavery.

Of the three songs which follow, the first was composed by Niklas Becker, about thirty years ago, on occasion of the alarm given to Europe, and specially to Germany, by the bellicose preparations and menaces of M. Thiers.[1] The second, the celebrated 'Wacht am Rhein,' came to life under the same Gallic provocation; and with regard to its authorship, as well as that of the music to which it is sung, we borrow the following account from the *Athenæum*:—

'It has now been clearly ascertained, beyond the shadow of a doubt, that "The Watch on the Rhine" was written in November 1840, a few months later than the famous "Rhine-Song," by Nicolaus Becker; and its author, who up to this time could not be named with any certainty, is Max Schneckenburger, a native of Thalheim, Würtemburg, who, as a young man of twenty or twenty-one, was then living at

---

[1] *Quarterly Review*, October 1870, p. 501.

Berne, and who, as has now been attested by the evidence of Professor Hundeshagen of Bonn, first read the verses, soon after they had been written, to a circle of German friends (Professor Hundeshagen being one of the number), then assembling occasionally at Burgdorf, near Berne. The song has been set to music several times (first in the " Chorliedersammlung für Schulen," by Erck and Greef), but only one tune—the one now universally adopted, and ringing through Germany and France, from the coastfires on the Baltic to the bivouacs of the Crown Prince of Prussia beyond Châlons — has become popular. It owes its origin to Carl Wilhelm, formerly Capellmeister at Crefeld, Rhenish Prussia, and dates as far back as some years before 1850. It was first made known by those celebrated part-singers the four brothers Steinhaus of Elberfeld, who sang it before the present King (then Prince) of Prussia, on the occasion of a *fête champêtre* given to him on the 6th July 1856, by the city of Elberfeld. Since then the song has become more and more a favourite with the choral unions of Germany, until, at the outbreak of the war, it suddenly became the favourite patriotic song,—in fact, *the* song of the whole German nation, superseding even the old national hymn of E. M. Arndt, " Was ist des Deutschen Vaterland ?" Carl Wilhelm, the composer of the song, now a man of about fifty years, is still living (although sick and in poverty), to earn the fruits of the sudden popularity of his tune. His name is on every tongue, the illustrated papers give his portrait, public subscriptions in his favour are successfully going on, and the Queen of Prussia has sent him a golden medal in acknowledgment of his merits. She had intended to confer the same honour on the poet, but poor Schneckenburger died young in 1851. His widow, who has corroborated Professor Hundeshagen's evidence by producing the original draft of the song in her late husband's handwriting, is still leading a quiet and retired life at Thalheim. His son is at present in the field, with the Würtemberg Jägers, in the army of the Crown Prince of Prussia.'

The third Rhine song, with which we conclude, is a popular air well known in this country, and generally sung to words instinct with the graceful beauty which belonged to the pen of Felicia Hemans; but for our present purpose it is more suitable to give a free translation of the original German words by Claudius.

The Rhine Boundary.

SIE SOLLEN IHN NICHT HABEN.

Melody VII.

The Rhine Boundary.

No! no! we'll keep our river,
  Our own, our German Rhine;
These foul-beaked ravens never
  Shall seize our glorious Rhine.

While, with broad bosom heaving,
  His mantle green he wears,
And while, his billows cleaving,
  The German boatman fares.

No! no! no Frankish master
  Shall hold our German Rhine,
While German hearts beat faster
  From his strong-hearted wine!

While mount is his, and meadow,
  And castle's rocky pride,
And mighty minster's shadow
  Floats on his ample tide.

No! no! they'll hold it never,
  While German staunch and true
Upon his German river
  A German maid shall woo!

While speckled fish is swimming
  His mighty flood below,
And German songs full-brimming
  From minstrel's mouth shall flow.

No! no! the sons of Hermann
  Will hold their own dear Rhine,
Until the last true German
  Lies buried 'neath the Rhine!

The Rhine Boundary.

DIE WACHT AM RHEIN.

Melody VIII.

C. Wilhelm.

The Rhine Boundary.

The Rhine Boundary.

Brave hearts and true shall watch, shall watch the Rhine.

A loud cry swells like thunder's peal,
Like roaring wave, like clashing steel :
The Rhine, the Rhine, the German Rhine !
Who 'll come to watch the German Rhine ?
    Dear fatherland, no fear be thine,
    Brave hearts and true shall watch the Rhine.

From heart to heart the quick thrill flies,
And lightning leaps from countless eyes,
Where each true German, sword in hand,
Guards the old border of the land.
    Dear fatherland, etc.

And though with Death he make his bed,
No stranger foot thy bank shall tread ;
Rich, as in waves thy regal flood,
Is Deutschland in true hero-blood.
    Dear fatherland, etc.

The Rhine Boundary.

He lifts his eye to Heaven's high crown,
Whence his high-hearted sires look down,
And swears an oath to keep thy flood
As German as his true heart's blood.
    Dear fatherland, etc.

Till the last drop shall drain our veins,
While in one arm one blade remains,
And while one fuming shot is sped,
No Frankish foot thy bank shall tread.
    Dear fatherland, etc.

The oath flies forth, the billows flow,
The forward banners flout the foe!
The Rhine, the Rhine, the German Rhine,
True Germans all, we watch the Rhine!
    Dear fatherland, no fear be thine,
    We watch, true Germans all, the Rhine!

The Rhine Boundary.

AM RHEIN, AM RHEIN, DA WACHSEN UNSRE REBEN.

MELODY IX.

The Rhine Boundary.

Come, crown your cups with leaves, your brows with
    garlands,
  And quaff the glowing wine!
No famous stream that rolls in near or far lands
  Gives blessings like the Rhine!

Not every vale of fruitful Deutschland bears it,
  The nectar-yielding vine;
On sunny slopes old Father Rhine prepares it,
  And yields this glowing wine.

The Brocken huge in shaggy length reclining
  Doth bear the giant pine,
Gives precious ore, gives berries bright and shining,
  But not this glowing wine.

True German wine we drink, not French or Spanish,
  When hand in hand we join,
And make our blood rich with the generous Rhenish
  Brewed by our German Rhine.

This noble wine it is both strong and mellow,
  And fires with strength divine:
Thus mild and strong be each true German fellow
  That loves our glorious Rhine!

God bless thy flood, thou regal-rolling river!
  We quaff thy glowing wine,
And, while we quaff, the Gaul shall claim thee never,
  Our own, our German Rhine!

So be it!—and may the songs which have been thus sung, and the blood which has been spilt, and the invasions which have been so manfully repelled, tend to produce in the British mind a lasting respect for that people to whose intellectual labours Europe has been under such great obligations, and whom we now at length, in insular Britain, see so much cause to admire, as our emulators and rivals in the world of policy and of action.

APPENDIX OF GERMAN WORDS TO THE MELODIES.

---

1. Es zog aus Berlin ein tapferer Held.

Es zog aus Berlin ein tapferer Held, juchhe!
Er führte sechshundert Reiter ins Feld, juchhe!
Sechshundert Reiter mit redlichem Muth,
Sie bürsteten alle Franzosen-blut,
    Juchhe, juchhe, juchhe,
      O Schill, dein Säbel thut weh!

Auch zogen mit Reitern und Rossen im Schritt
Wohl tausend der tapfersten Schützen mit.
Ihr Schützen, Gott segne euch jeglichen Schuß,
Durch welchen ein Franzmann erblassen muß!
    Juchhe, etc.

So ziehet der tapfere, der muthige Schill,
Der mit den Franzosen sich schlagen will;
Ihn sendet kein Kaiser, kein König aus,
Ihn sendet die Freiheit, das Vaterland aus.
    Juchhe, etc.

Bei Dodendorf färbten die Männer gut
Das fette Land mit Französischem Blut,
Zwei tausend zerhieben die Säbel blank,
Die übrigen machten die Beine lang.
    Juchhe, etc.

Drauf stürmten sie Dömitz, das feste Haus,
Und jagten die Schelmenfranzosen hinaus,
Dann zogen sie lustig in's Pommerland ein,
Da soll kein Franzose sein Kirri mehr schrei'n.
    Juchhe, etc.

Auf Stralsund stürmte der reisige Zug—
O, Franzosen, verstündet ihr Vogelflug!
O, wüchsen euch Federn und Flügel geschwind!
Es nahet der Schill und er reitet wie Wind.
    Juchhe, etc.

Er reitet wie Wetter hinein in die Stadt,
Wo der Wallenstein weiland verlegen sich hat,

Wo der zwölfte Karolus im Thore schlief;
Jetzt liegen ihre Thürme und Mauern tief.
  Juchhe, etc.

O, weh euch, Franzosen! wie mäht der Tod!
Wie färben die Reiter die Säbel roth!
Die Reiter, sie fühlen das deutsche Blut,
Franzosen zu tödten, das däucht ihnen gut.
  Juchhe, etc.

O, wehe dir, Schill! Du tapferer Held!
Was sind dir für bübische Netze gestellt!
Viel ziehen zu Lande, es schleichet vom Meer
Der Däne, die tückische Schlange daher.
  Juchhe, etc.

O Schill! O Schill, du tapferer Held!
Was sprengest du nicht mit den Reitern in's Feld?
Was schließt du in Mauern die Tapferkeit ein?
Bei Stralsund sollst du begraben sein!
  Juchhe, etc.

O Stralsund! O trauriges Stralesund!
In dir geht das tapferste Herz zu Grund;
Eine Kugel durchbohret das redlichste Herz,
Und Buben, sie treiben mit Helden Scherz.
  Juchhe, etc.

Da schreit ein frecher Franzosenmund:
Man soll ihn begraben wie einen Hund,
Wie einen Schelm, der an Galgen und Rad
Schon fütterte Krähen und Raben satt.
 Juchhe, etc.

So trugen sie ihn ohne Sang und Klang,
Ohne Pfeifengetön, ohne Trommelklang,
Ohne Kanonenmusik, ohne Flintengruß,
Womit man den Wehrmann begraben muß.
 Juchhe, etc.

Sie schnitten den Kopf von dem Rumpfe ihm ab,
Und warfen den Leib in ein schlechtes Grab;
Da liegt er nun bis an den jüngsten Tag,
Wo Gott ihn in Freuden erwecken mag.
 Juchhe, etc.

Da schläft nun der fromme, der tapfere Held,
Ihm ward kein Stein zum Gedächtniß gestellt;
Doch hat er gleich keinen Ehrenstein,
Sein Name wird nimmer vergessen sein.
 Juchhe, etc.

Denn sattelt ein Reiter sein schnelles Pferd,
Und schwinget ein Reiter sein blankes Schwert,
So rufet er zornig, Herr Schill! Herr Schill!
Ich an den Franzosen euch rächen will.
 Juchhe, etc.

2. Was ist des Deutschen Vaterland?

Was ist des Deutschen Vaterland?
Ist's Preußenland? ist's Schwabenland?
Ist's wo am Rhein die Rebe blüht?
Ist's wo am Belt die Möve zieht!
    O nein! nein! nein!
    Sein Vaterland muß größer sein,
    Sein Vaterland muß größer sein.

Was ist des Deutschen Vaterland?
Ist's Baierland? ist's Steierland?
Gewiß es ist das Oesterreich,
An Siegen und an Ehren reich!
    O nein! nein! nein! etc.

Was ist des Deutschen Vaterland?
Ist's Pommerland? Westphalenland?
Ist's wo der Sand der Dünen weht?
Ist's wo die Donau brausend geht?
    O nein! nein! nein! etc.

Was ist des Deutschen Vaterland?
So nenne mir das große Land?
Ist's Land der Schweizer, ist's Tirol?
Das Land und Volk gefiel mir wohl!
    Doch nein! nein! nein!
    Sein Vaterland muß größer sein,
    Sein Vaterland muß größer sein.

Was ist des Deutschen Vaterland?
So nenne endlich mir das Land!
„So weit die deutsche Zunge klingt,
Und Gott im Himmel Lieder singt."
 Das soll es sein, das soll es sein!
 Das, wackrer Deutscher, nenne Dein,
 Das nenne Dein.

Das ganze Deutschland soll es sein,
O Gott vom Himmel sieh darein!
Und gieb uns ächten deutschen Muth,
Daß wir es lieben treu und gut.
 Das soll es sein, das soll es sein,
 Das ganze Deutschland soll es sein, das soll
  es sein,
 Das ganze Deutschland soll es sein.

3. Was blasen die Trompeten?

Was blasen die Trompeten? Husaren heraus!
Es reitet der Feldmarschall im fliegenden Saus!
Er reitet so freudig sein muthiges Pferd,
Er schwinget so schneidig sein blitzendes Schwert,
 Juchhei rassassa! und die Deutschen sind da,
 Die Deutschen sind lustig, sie rufen: hurrah!

O schauet, wie ihm leuchten die Augen so klar;
O schauet wie ihm wallet sein schneeweißes Haar!

So frisch blüht sein Alter, wie greisender Wein,
Drum kann er auch Verwalter des Schlachtfeld's sein.
    Juchhei rassassa! etc.

Er ist der Mann gewesen, als Alles versank,
Der muthig auf zum Himmel den Degen noch schwang.
Da schwur er beim Eisen gar zornig und hart,
Dem Franzmann zu weisen die deutsche Art.
    Juchhei rassassa! etc.

Den Schwur hat er gehalten, als Kriegsruf erklang,
Hei! wie der weiße Jüngling im Sattel sich schwang!
Da ist er's gewesen, der Kehraus gemacht,
Mit eisernem Besen das Land rein gemacht.
    Juchhei rassassa! etc.

Bei Lützen auf der Aue, da hielt er solchen Strauß,
Daß vielen tausend Welschen der Athem ging aus,
Daß Tausende liefen gar hastigen Lauf,
Zehntausend entschliefen, die nimmer wachen auf.
    Juchhei rassassa! etc.

Bei Katzbach an dem Wasser, da hat er's auch bewährt,
Da hat er den Franzosen das schwimmen gelehrt.
Fahrt wohl, ihr Franzosen, zur Ostsee hinab,
Und nehmet, ohnehosen, den Wallfisch zum Grab.
    Juchhei rassassa! etc.

Bei Wartenburg an der Elbe, wie fuhr er da hindurch!
Da schirmte die Franzosen nicht Schanze, nicht Burg.
Sie mußten wieder springen, wie Hasen über's Feld,
Und hinterdrein ließ klingen sein Hussa der Held.
   Juchhei rassassa! etc.

Bei Leipzig auf dem Plane, o schöne Ehrenschlacht!
Da brach er den Franzosen in Trümmer Glück und Macht,
Da lagen sie so sicher nach letztem harten Fall,
Da ward der alte Blücher ein Feldmarschall.
   Juchhei rassassa! etc.

Drum blaset, ihr Trompeten, Husaren heraus.
Du, reite, Herr Feldmarschall, wie Sturmwind im Saus!
Dem Siege entgegen zum Rhein, über'n Rhein!
Du alter tapf'rer Degen, in Frankreich hinein!
   Juchhei rassassa! etc.

4. Was glänzt dort vom Walde?

Was glänzt dort vom Walde im Sonnenschein?
Hör's näher und näher brausen.
Es zieht sich herunter in düsteren Reih'n
Und gellende Hörner erschallen darein,
Erfüllen die Seele mit Grausen.
Und wenn ihr die schwarzen Gesellen fragt:
Das ist, das ist Lützow's wilde verwegene Jagd!

Was zieht dort rasch durch den finstern Wald,
Und streifet von Bergen zu Bergen?
Es legt sich in nächtlichen Hinterhalt,
Das Hurrah jauchzt und die Büchse knallt,
Es fallen die fränkischen Schergen.
Und wenn ihr die schwarzen Jäger fragt:
Das ist, das ist Lützow's wilde verwegene Jagd!

Wo die Reben dort glühen, dort braust der Rhein,
Der Wüthrich geborgen sich meinte;
Da naht es schnell mit Gewitterschein
Und wirft sich mit rüstigen Armen hinein,
Und springet an's Ufer der Feinde.
Und wenn ihr die schwarzen Schwimmer fragt:
Das ist, das ist Lützow's wilde verwegene Jagd!

Was braust dort im Thale die wilde Schlacht,
Was schlagen die Schwerter zusammen?
Hochherzige Reiter schlagen die Schlacht,
Und der Funke der Freiheit ist glühend erwacht
Und lobert in blutigen Flammen!
Und wenn ihr die schwarzen Reiter fragt:
Das ist Lützow's wilde verwegene Jagd!

Wer scheidet dort röchelnd vom Sonnenlicht,
Unter winselnde Feinde gebettet?

Es zucket der Tod auf dem Angesicht:
Doch die wackern Herzen erzittern nicht,
Das Vaterland ist ja gerettet!
Und wenn ihr die schwarzen Gefall'nen fragt:
Das ist Lützow's, wilde verwegene Jagd!

Die wilde Jagd, und die deutsche Jagd
Auf Henkersblut und Tyrannen!
Drum, die ihr uns liebt, nicht geweint uns geklagt!
Das Land ist ja frei und der Morgen tagt,
Wenn wir's auch nur sterbend gewannen!
Und von Enkeln zu Enkeln sei's nachgesagt:
Das war Lützow's wilde, verwegene Jagd!

5. Vater, ich rufe dich.

Vater, ich rufe dich!
Brüllend umwölkt mich der Dampf der Geschütze,
Sprühend umzucken mich rasselnde Blitze;
Lenker der Schlachten, ich rufe dich,
Vater, du führe mich!

Vater, du führe mich!
Führ' mich zum Siege, führ' mich zum Tode!
Herr, ich erkenne deine Gebote;
Herr, wie du willst, so führe mich!
Gott, ich erkenne dich!

Gott, ich erkenne dich!
So im herbstlichen Rauschen der Blätter,
Als im Schlachtendonnerwetter
Urquell der Gnade, erkenn' ich dich!
Vater, du segne mich.

Vater, du segne mich!
In deine Hand befehl' ich mein Leben!
Du kannst es nehmen, du hast es gegeben;
Zum Leben, zum Sterben segne mich!
Vater, ich preise dich!

Vater, ich preise dich!
'S ist ja kein Kampf für die Güter der Erde
Das Heiligste schützen wir mit dem Schwerte!
D'rum, fallend und siegend, preis' ich dich!
Gott, dir ergeb' ich mich!

Gott, dir ergeb' ich mich!
Wenn mich die Donner des Todes begrüßen,
Wenn meine Adern geöffnet fließen:
Dir, mein Gott, dir ergeb' ich mich!
Vater, ich rufe dich!

6. Du Schwert an meiner Linken.

Du Schwert an meiner Linken,
Was soll dein freundlich Blinken?

Schaust mich so freundlich an,
Hab' meine Freude dran.
    Hurrah! Hurrah! Hurrah!

„Mich trägt ein wackrer Reiter,
Drum blink' ich auch so heiter;
Bin frei'n Mannes Wehr,
Das freut dem Schwerte sehr."
    Hurrah! etc.

Ja gutes Schwert, frei bin ich
Und liebe dich herzinnig,
Als wärst du mir getraut,
Als eine liebe Braut.
    Hurrah! etc.

„Dir hab' ich's ja ergeben,
Mein lichtes Eisenleben.
Ach, wären wir getraut!
Wann holst du deine Braut?"
    Hurrah! etc.

Zur Brautnachts=Morgenröthe
Ruft festlich die Trompete;
Wenn die Kanonen schrei'n,
Hol' ich das Liebchen ein.
    Hurrah! etc.

„O seliges Umfangen!
Ich harre mit Verlangen.
Du, Bräut'gam, hole mich,
Mein Kränzchen bleibt für dich."
    Hurrah! etc.

Was klirrst du in der Scheide,
Du helle Eisenfreude,
So wild, so schlachtenfroh.
Mein Schwert, was klirrst du so?
    Hurrah! etc.

„Wohl klirr' ich in der Scheide,
Ich sehne mich zum Streite,
Recht wild und schlachtenfroh.
Drum Reiter, klirr' ich so."
    Hurrah! etc.

Bleib' doch im engen Stübchen;
Was willst du hier, mein Liebchen?
Bleib still im Kämmerlein;
Bleib, bald hol' ich dich ein.
    Hurrah! etc.

„Laß mich nicht lange warten
O schöner Liebesgarten,
Voll Röslein blutigroth,
Und aufgeblühtem Tod."
    Hurrah! etc.

So komm denn aus der Scheide,
Du, Reiters Augenweide.
Heraus, mein Schwert, heraus!
Führ' dich in's Vaterhaus.
 Hurrah! etc.

„Ach herrlich ist's im Freien,
Im rüst'gen Hochzeitsreihen.
Wie glänzt im Sonnenstrahl
So bräutlich hell der Stahl!"
 Hurrah! etc.

Wohlauf! ihr kecken Streiter!
Wohlauf! ihr deutschen Reiter!
Wird euch das Herz nicht warm?
Nehmt's Liebchen in den Arm.
 Hurrah! etc.

Erst that es an der Linken
Nur ganz verstohlen blinken;
Doch an die Rechte traut
Gott sichtbarlich die Braut.
 Hurrah! etc.

Drum drückt den liebeheißen,
Bräutlichen Mund von Eisen

An eure Lippen fest!
Fluch! wer die Braut verläßt.
	Hurrah! etc.

Nun laßt das Liebchen singen,
Daß helle Funken springen!
Der Hochzeitmorgen graut.—
Hurrah, du Eisenbraut.
	Hurrah! etc.

7. Sie sollen ihn nicht haben.

Sie sollen ihn nicht haben, den freien deutschen Rhein,
Ob sie wie gier'ge Raben sich heisser darnach schrein;

So lang' er ruhig wallend sein grünes Kleid noch trägt,
So lang' ein Ruder schallend an seine Wogen schlägt.

Sie sollen ihn nicht haben, den freien deutschen Rhein,
So lang' sich Herzen laben an seinem Feuerwein;

So lang' in seinem Strome noch fest die Felsen stehn,
So lang' sich hohe Dome in seinem Spiegel sehn.

Sie sollen ihn nicht haben, den freien deutschen Rhein,
So lang' dort kühne Knaben um schlanke Dirnen frein;

So lang' die Floſſe hebet ein Fiſch auf ſeinem Grund,
So lang' ein Lied noch lebet in ſeiner Sänger Mund.

Sie ſollen ihn nicht haben, den freien deutſchen Rhein,
Bis ſeine Fluth begraben des letzten Manns Gebein!

8. Die Wacht am Rhein.

Es brauſt ein Ruf wie Donnerhall,
Wie Schwertgeklirr und Wogenprall:
Zum Rhein, zum Rhein, zum deutſchen Rhein,
Wer will des Stromes Hüter ſein!
    Lieb Vaterland, magſt ruhig ſein,
    Lieb Vaterland, magſt ruhig ſein;
    Feſt ſteht und treu die Wacht, die Wacht am Rhein!
    Feſt ſteht und treu die Wacht, die Wacht am Rhein!

Durch Hunderttauſend zuckt es ſchnell,
Und Aller Augen blitzen hell,
Der Deutſche bieder, fromm und ſtark,
Beſchützt die heil'ge Landes=Mark.
    Lieb Vaterland, etc.

Er blickt hinauf in Himmelsau'n,
Da Helden=Väter niederſchau'n,
Und ſchwört mit ſtolzer Kampfesluſt:
„Du Rhein bleibſt deutſch wie meine Bruſt!"
    Lieb Vaterland, etc.

So lang ein Tropfen Blut noch glüht,
Noch eine Faust den Degen zieht,
Und noch ein Arm die Büchse spannt,
Betritt kein Feind hier deinen Strand!
    Lieb Vaterland, etc.

Der Schwur erschallt, die Wogen rinnt,
Die Fahnen flattern hoch im Wind,
Am Rhein, am Rhein, am deutschen Rhein,
Wir alle wollen Hüter sein!
    Lieb Vaterland, etc.

9. Am Rhein, am Rhein, da wachsen.

Am Rhein, am Rhein, da wachsen unsre Reben,
Gesegnet sei der Rhein, gesegnet sei der Rhein!
Da wachsen sie am Ufer hin und geben
Uns diesen Labewein, uns diesen Labewein,
Uns diesen Labewein, uns diesen Labewein.

So trinkt! so trinkt! und laßt uns allewege
Uns freu'n und fröhlich sein, uns freu'n und fröhlich sein,
Und wüßten wir, wo Jemand traurig läge,
Wir gäben ihm den Wein, wir gäben ihm den Wein,
Wir gäben ihm den Wein, wir gäben ihm den Wein.

www.ingramcontent.com/pod-product-compliance
Lightning Source LLC
Chambersburg PA
CBHW030314170426
43202CB00009B/1001